Explorations in Language Study
General Editors:
Peter Doughty   Geoffrey Thornton

LANGUAGE STUDY, THE TEACHER AND THE LEARNER

**Peter Doughty
and
Geoffrey Thornton**

EDWARD ARNOLD

© Peter Doughty and Geoffrey Thornton 1973

First published 1973
by Edward Arnold (Publishers) Ltd.
25 Hill Street London W1X 8LL

ISBN 0 7131 1755 9

Explorations in Language Study

Language Study, the Teacher and the Learner
P. S. Doughty and G. M. Thornton

Explorations in the Functions of Language
M. A. K. Halliday

English as a Second and Foreign Language
B. Harrison

In Preparation

Language in the Junior School
E. Ashworth

Language and Community
P. S. and E. A. Doughty

Language, Brain and Interactive Processes
R. S. Gurney

Language in Bi-lingual Communities
D. Sharp

Language, Experience and School
G. M. Thornton

Printed in Great Britain by Butler & Tanner Ltd,
Frome and London

Contents

General Introduction

In the course of our efforts to develop a linguistic focus for work in English language, now published as *Language in Use*, we came to realize the extent of the growing interest in what we would call a linguistic approach to language. Lecturers in Colleges and Departments of Education see the relevance of such an approach in the education of teachers. Many teachers in schools and in colleges of Further Education see themselves that 'Educational failure is primarily *linguistic* failure', and have turned to Linguistic Science for some kind of exploration and practical guidance. Many of those now exploring the problems of relationships, community or society, from a sociological or psychological point of view wish to make use of a linguistic approach to the language in so far as it is relevant to these problems.

We were conscious of the wide divergence between the aims of the linguist, primarily interested in language as a system for organizing 'meanings', and the needs of those who now wanted to gain access to the insights that resulted from that interest. In particular, we were aware of the wide gap that separated the literature of academic Linguistics from the majority of those who wished to find out what Linguistic Science might have to say about language and the use of language.

Out of this experience emerged our own view of that much used term, 'Language Study', developed initially in the chapters of *Exploring Language*, and now given expression in this series. Language Study is not a subject, but a process, which is why the series is to be called *Explorations in Language Study*. Each exploration is focused upon a meeting point between the insights of Linguistic Science, often in conjunction with other social sciences, and the linguistic questions raised by the study of a particular aspect of individual behaviour or human society.

Initially, the volumes in the series have a particular relevance

5

to the role of language in teaching and learning. The editors intend that they should make a basic contribution to the literature of Language Study, doing justice equally to the findings of the academic disciplines involved and the practical needs of those who now want to take a linguistic view of their own particular problems of language and the use of language.

Peter Doughty
Geoffrey Thornton

Part I
The Concept of Language Study
by
Peter Doughty

1 The nature of the need

1. A new focus on language

In the summer of 1971, over seven hundred teachers, academics, advisers, inspectors and educational administrators gathered together at the University of York, England. They had come from the United States, Canada and Great Britain to take part in an international conference on the teaching and learning of English. It might seem to many teachers that a major gathering of people concerned with one single subject could have very little relevance for those who teach any other subject. This was not the case, however. Interest and discussion moved away from a narrow concern with the practice of 'English' and took up a new focus, the part played by *language*, not just in 'English', but in all teaching and learning. As the conference went on, moreover, it proved impossible to focus upon language in teaching and learning without considering, at the same time, the part played by language in shaping the lives of men and the fabric of their societies.

The people who met at York brought with them an enormous diversity of educational experience, which ranged from the nursery group to the post-graduate seminar, with learners of all ages and levels of ability. They combined a similarly wide range of experience in the area of organization and administration, from the problems of running a small department to the complexities of planning educational policy for a large state. Above all, they were people who had come to the conference because their individual experience had led them to ask questions about many aspects of what is now done in the name of education. They met to talk about the practice of their trade as teachers of 'English' and discovered in the process that it only made sense to do so as long as they were willing to focus upon all learners as, first and foremost,

9

users of language. By reaching this conclusion, they recognized the inescapable fact that it is language that is the critically determining factor in pupils' capacity to learn.

On the last day of the conference, in a final plenary session which gave expression to the sense of the meeting, it was agreed,

To redefine our subject in the light of the language needs of all children and their probable needs in a kind of society we cannot predict.

Many teachers might react to this statement of aim by suggesting that it was about time teachers of English looked to their responsibilities, and many others outside the educational system would echo their sentiments. Implicit in this reaction is the familiar idea that '. . . the language needs of all children . . .' can and ought to be met by the work of the English Department. The conference resolution might seem to suggest that a new age was heralded in which pupils would turn up for every class, ready and able to use whatever spoken or written language was required of them by the subject teacher concerned.

If we look at the resolution a little more closely, however, we will find that its implications do not point that way at all. Certainly, the resolution *does* reaffirm the central part to be played by language in the work of English Departments. It does not imply, however, that those who teach 'English' should carry *sole* responsibility for the learner's operational command of language, written or spoken. In order to bring the work of the English Department into line with the sense of the resolution, there would certainly have to be a very sharp focus upon '. . . the language needs of all children . . .'. This means that we need to be much more sharply aware of how they arise, what determines their character, and who would be best able to meet them. It also means that we need to look at a whole range of current class-room practices and ask how they relate to this central question of language need. It would only be possible to answer these questions, however, if we were willing to look at the way in which all teachers and all subjects create language needs particular to themselves. This implies that some redefinition, along the lines of the resolution, will be required for all subjects, if all teachers recognize the part played by language in their own class-rooms.

In particular, an appropriate redefinition of 'English' could not get very far without exploring the basic question of pupils' command of a language, written and spoken. This would lead us to distinguish between the general contribution the teacher of English can make towards this command and the particular contribution that has to come from every teacher in terms of the language needs of his own situation. We would have to look at the ways in which other aspects of the life of the school could affect its pupils' capacity to use language for learning. Such matters as the school's pattern of discipline, its customary view of relationships between teachers and pupils, the relationships it permits between pupils of different age groups or sexes, its attitude towards pupils' everyday speech, all these help to create the climate for language use within each individual class-room. As teachers, we can only show a properly professional approach to '. . . the language needs of all children . . .', therefore, if we are prepared to examine the whole network of relationships between teachers, pupils, subjects and language that go to make up a school. It is the purpose of this book to show how a linguistic approach to the language needs and the language problems of teachers and pupils might enable us to carry out this examination.

2. Terms for discussion

Writing about the field of education presents one particularly acute problem. Almost everyone goes to school; many people go on being involved with schools as parents or as employers; and so talk about education is part of ordinary, everyday life. The result of this is that there are a very large number of words and phrases about education and its processes constantly in use as part of the common language. These words and phrases, moreover, embody our habitual ways of thinking about schools and colleges, teachers and lecturers, pupils and students, and so on. When words and phrases have this sort of function, however, the range of meanings they express can be very wide.

Each person is likely to have his or her own version of what they really mean, and precision is lost through their very accessibility.

If the object of a book is to explore a new approach to established subjects, or new directions in the curriculum, then this can scarcely be done without presenting a challenge to received ideas as to what some of those words and phrases mean, because explorations of this kind will necessarily call into question the habitual ways of thinking that they express. For instance, what needs to be said about language as a function of teaching and learning will very often apply to *all* learning situations, wherever they occur. This is because the things that we have to say are derived from a *general* consideration of the nature and function of language. To couch our argument in terms of the particular divisions and boundaries within the curriculum and the educational process as we know it would merely obscure and distort the value of what a linguistic approach to language in teaching and learning can offer.

The need to cut across boundaries is well illustrated by pairs of words like schools and colleges, teachers and lecturers, pupils and students. In dividing up our world we mark the boundaries we draw by attaching linguistic labels to them. In time we come to think of these boundaries as somehow a part of nature, because we use different words for whatever we place on alternative sides of the boundaries we draw. Moreover, what people normally use to carry on everyday conversation, the common language, very often reinforces this habit of mind, because the common language does not contain words or phrases which readily embrace elements on either side of such boundaries. Consider this group—teacher, pupil, school: and now this—lecturer, student, college. What words and phrases are there to express the common elements which underly both sets of words and yet retain the status of a common language expression? The answer is that there aren't any. If, therefore, we want to point to what schools and colleges, teachers and lecturers, pupils and students have in common, because they are all involved in one process of education, then we shall have to use new terms.

There is a proper scepticism amongst those involved in education, however, about the proliferating terminology of educational studies. Many teachers believe that there is no practical value to be gained by using the new terms these studies introduce. Consider, however, the implications of the following example, taken from the correspondence columns of a leading national daily newspaper, noted for its interest in social questions. One reader wrote to complain about what he regarded as ". . . the terrible jargon the social scientists are at present inflicting upon us". His point was that he had been asked in the street to contribute money for the aid of 'underprivileged children', which he regarded as an 'awful synonym for poor kids'. In reply to his letter, a social scientist pointed out that these terms were by no means synonomous. He said that,

> . . . the term underprivileged assigns responsibility to its rightful owners—the privileged. On the other hand, the term poor . . .

leaves responsibility open, thereby providing people the let out of assigning responsibility for poverty to the poor themselves. Now the value of this example is that it comes from the market-place. The person who was doing the collecting wanted to express a theory about why poor children are poor, and the term 'under-privileged' does express an underlying body of ideas about why people are poor. The common language phrase, 'poor kids', however, is loosely descriptive and expressive. It is important to see that the use of a term like 'underprivileged' *does* express a point of view, one version of the facts, and it allows us to dispute this version of the facts because the version has been made explicit. The two phrases, 'poor kids' and 'underprivileged children', in fact belong to very different types of discourse, and consequently they give rise to very different styles of discussion. Put bluntly, every man is free to argue his own view of why kids are poor, but disagreement about the underprivileged must make some reference to the facts.

Terms are most needed precisely where their use is likely to cause most irritation, where the subject in question belongs, and has always belonged, in the market-place. Just as the poor are always with us, and therefore have always been a subject for discussion between ordinary members of the community, so have schools and pupils and education. The particular example of the underprivileged is closely paralleled by the familiar educational question of 'ability'. Saying 'dull kids', 'weak pupils', 'the not-so-bright ones', is the equivalent of saying 'poor kids'. These phrases imply many things about our habitual cultural attitudes towards learning, but they do not express a *theory*. Their use does not demand of us a rational and ordered response which takes account of the facts. If we talk about 'the culturally deprived', 'the less able', 'the average pupil', however, we *do* assert a theory and may be properly challenged to state our reasons for taking this view of the facts rather than any of the possible alternative views available to us.

This book, therefore, and those that follow it in this series, ought to use terms that clearly reveal their author's view of the facts. What they say needs to be taken up and challenged, because the explorations that they offer are new. The aim of the series is to provide a basis for discussion, and disagreement, and therefore to stimulate development of the ideas involved.

Let me illustrate this argument by looking at the key phrase in the York conference resolution, 'the language needs of all

13

children'. The use of the word 'children' in this phrase might lead one to think that only those up to the age of nine or ten were being referred to. This book, however, is concerned with all those involved in the educational process from nursery school to college. Its focus is upon the language needs of all *learners*, whatever their situation, age or intellectual ability.

Using *learner* in this way reminds us again of the boundaries built into our thinking by pairs of words like school and college, teacher and lecturer, pupil and student. As teachers, our own situation in the class-room makes us so conscious of the *differences* between learning situations that we lose sight of what they have in common. By using the term *learner* to cover everyone who enters into a learning situation *in order to learn*, whether child, adolescent, or adult, pupil or student, average or able, we are pointing to what they all have in common as learners, *the particular language needs which arise from the learning situation in which they find themselves.* All those, therefore, who enter into the learning situation in order to impart, instruct, lead, organize, guide, or otherwise interact with learners we must call *teachers*.

3. Schools and colleges: institutions or agencies?

The everyday use of language sets up in our minds boundaries between schools and colleges, and between different kinds of school, Nursery and Infant, Infant and Junior, Junior and Secondary. We tend to speak about these different kinds of school as though each one of them accommodates a type of learner *totally distinct in all respects* from any other. By using the term *educational system* we can point to what they all share in common because they are agencies established for the formal transmission of knowledge, intellectual and social and cultural, from one generation to the next.

This use of the word *agency*, rather than institution, is one more example of choosing a term because one particular view of the facts is being advanced rather than another. To talk about schools and colleges as institutions points to their discreteness, their individual autonomy, the fact that they exist as buildings, bricks and mortar, glass and concrete and steel. Institutions are things and they have fixed limits. Where one institution ends, and another begins, is 'obvious'. Consequently it is easy to consider them in terms of their rights and privileges, their spheres of influence and so on. The word institution, therefore, implies a theory

14

about the educational system in which schools and colleges exist independently of anything else and treat with each other as sovereign bodies. But such a view of the educational system will not help us if we need to focus upon the function of language in teaching and learning, wherever teaching and learning occurs.

To talk about schools and colleges as *educational agencies*, on the other hand, implies a very different theory about the educational system. What this view of schools and colleges suggests is the fact that they are not so much buildings, scholastic or administrative units, as collections of people, using certain means to achieve particular educational ends. The word 'agency' points to a theory in which schools and colleges only exist in so far as societies and individuals have need of them. They are so intimately related to the society in which they exist that there is no real sense in which they can be thought of as autonomous. The boundaries of educational agencies are much less easily defined because the essence of their function is to mediate between learners and bodies of knowledge, intellectual and social and cultural. If educational institutions are isolates with impermeable boundaries, then educational agencies are locations for social processes.

All schools and colleges, then, share the task of relaying certain aspects of the culture of their society to those individuals who are in the process of becoming new members of it. 'Culture', in this case, is not to be read as the high culture of the humanist, Arnold's '. . . the best that has been thought and said . . .', but rather what has been so well described by Sir Edward Tyler, the British anthropologist, as,

> . . . that complex whole which includes knowledge, belief, art, morals, law, custom, and any other capabilities and habits acquired by man as a member of society.

If schools and colleges are concerned with the process of mediating between the existing store of '. . . capabilities and habits . . .', and those who are in the process of acquiring them in order to become fully-fledged members of that society, then we are more interested in their mediatory role than in their rights and privileges.

As institutions, schools and colleges appear free to pursue their own ends, and are conscious of the need to maintain their individual identity by a rigorous defence of the boundaries that separate them from each other and from the rest of society; as agencies, however, their focus must be upon the process that relates culture to individual learners, a process that necessarily involves the crossing of many boundaries.

4. The 'needs' of learners

The use of the word 'need' in our key phrase, '. . . the language needs of all children . . .' is a perfect demonstration of the difficulties that arise when we use a familiar word from the common language, and do not set out the particular meaning we intend it to carry. At the present time, as we use it in educational discussion, 'need' is doubly ambiguous, so that we should be particularly careful to distinguish our intended meaning when we do use it.

On the one hand, our use of the word expresses either a concern for the child's personal development as an individual sentient self or a focus upon his parallel development as a social self, a creature made by and through his continuous contact with other human beings. Perhaps we might expect that these two ways of interpreting the word really amount to the same thing, as far as the child's experience of the world is concerned. That this ambiguity has arisen is an indication of the degree to which we feel that this is no longer the case in an advanced industrial society like ours. From the point of view of the educational system, moreover, this ambiguity is reflected in a divergence of emphasis that is vitally important for the language needs of all learners. Those who believe that 'needs' refer primarily to the development of the personal self are likely to emphasize the imaginative and individually creative aspects of language activity, while those who think of 'needs' primarily in terms of the capacity to make relationships with others are likely to stress the public and social aspects of language activity.

On the other hand, we use 'need' to refer either to what society demands of its members, or to what the educational system demands of those who are involved in it as learners. In this case, the ambiguity arises because schools and colleges exist to provide what is *needed* for survival in a particular society, and, at the same time, create their own needs in the process. From the point of view of the language needs of all learners, this ambiguity leads to a blurring of focus as to what kinds of languaging activity ought to be set up in learning situations and for what purposes. There is a divergence between those who think of 'needs' in terms of the kinds of language activity society expects of pupils and students, *because they have been through the formal educational system*; and those

16

who think in terms of the use of language they require of pupils and students, *because they are pupils and students.*

Unfortunately, the way language works encourages us to treat any two somethings, like the two meanings of an ambiguity, as quite separate from each other in every respect, once we have distinguished them. Neither of the pairs of meanings which I have just described ought to be read in this way, however. The distinction between the personal, and the social, needs of the child is clearly a question of the focus. From either point of view, the personal or the social, the focus is upon the developing self of the individual child. The ambiguity only arises because we can view this development, and therefore our assessment of the needs that follow from it, either from a standpoint *inside* the circle of the child's autonomous self, looking out towards the world at large, or from a standpoint *outside* that circle, looking in on it from the direction of the network of demands that the world makes upon him.

The second pair of meanings, the distinction between the needs of society and of the educational system, show a different kind of relationship. In this case, the needs arising from the learner's participation in the educational system are but one example of the needs which arise because he lives in society. We can put this more formally by saying that his needs as a learner are but a sub-set of the whole set of needs that living in a human community gives rise to.

This distinction has a particular significance for the language needs of learners, and leads me to use the terms *language for learning* and *language for living*. *Language for living* will refer to all the ways in which human beings make use of language in the ordinary course of their everyday lives; and *language for learning* will refer to all the ways in which language enters into the process of teaching and learning. A proper understanding of the relationship between *language for living* and *language for learning* is vital to a coherent theory of Language Study. Unless we see clearly the ways in which language for learning relates to, and derives from, language for living, we will never be able to make sense of the language needs of the learners, nor the linguistic problems that face all teachers.

2 Cultural attitudes, language and the learning situation

1. Linguistic perspectives and socialization

We now have so clear a picture of the crucial part played by language in learning that no teacher can really afford to overlook or ignore or leave to others the way in which his own pupils use language to learn. This situation demands an appropriate linguistic perspective towards language which would be available to every teacher for looking at the practical problems of his own situation. Such a perspective would become an essential element in the professional competence of a teacher, in the same way as the teaching of reading is now considered to be an essential element in the professional competence of all first school teachers or a knowledge of the discipline is considered to be an essential element in the professional competence of all subject specialist teachers.

This perspective cannot come from an individual's ordinary everyday acquaintance with language, however, or even from his traditional professional concern with it as a teacher. What is required is a form of Language Study specifically developed to meet the needs of those who are involved in the process of education *as teachers*. Given the nature of the need, and the uniqueness of language as a subject for study, together with the fact that it is the personal possession of everyone who takes up such a study, an appropriate form for it is not going to be easy to find. About the only thing that can be said with absolute certainty is that it will not look anything like the customary pattern of an academic 'subject matter'. Why this should be so is properly the concern of the rest of this book, but perhaps it would be useful at this stage in the argument to outline briefly the sort of consideration which has led to this conclusion. It seems to me that in devising an

18

approach to Language Study there are four matters in particular that no one can properly afford to ignore.

Firstly, there is the fact that questions about language activity in real situations, like homes and shops and factories and classrooms, do not readily yield to enquiries conducted exclusively within the boundaries of a single discipline. An appropriate form for Language Study is therefore going to have to be interdisciplinary. Then there is the fact that the development of a linguistic perspective will make considerable demands upon individual teachers, because it will require them to modify their existing assumptions about language and attitudes towards its use. Modifying one's attitudes and assumptions is never an easy matter, and those that we hold in respect of language we hold most tenaciously, because many of them have been acquired as a result of growing up in a particular community, or even indeed as part of the actual process of acquiring language itself. They are therefore a very intimate, if non-explicit, part of our way of viewing the world. We must be able to put forward arguments for a new perspective in such a way that people will not feel their existing attitudes and assumptions are under attack, and therefore need defending, but be encouraged to rethink them in the light of the new understanding Language Study has to offer.

A third consideration is more daunting. If this case for Language Study is valid, it is clear that when one says that a linguistic perspective is a vital part of the professional competence of all teachers, then, at present, the vast majority of those whom one wants to involve in Language Study are going to be experienced practising teachers. They do not have the time, nor do most governments have the resources to provide, for a long period of detailed academic study. What is needed is rather a means of developing a way of thinking about particular issues, a way of conducting particular enquiries, than anything that could be pointed to as a recognizable 'body of knowledge'. 'Knowing the facts' is much less important in this context than knowing what questions to ask and what the answers to those questions might conceivably look like.

There is one more consideration to bring in at this stage. I have spoken about '. . . a form of study specifically developed to meet the needs of those who are involved in the process of education *as teachers*'. There are, of course, two participants in that process, for learners also have needs. Language Study must therefore develop a dual focus. In other words, one essential aspect of Language

Study is to show how a linguistic perspective can relate to the particular needs of all learners. It must also be ready to show how the learner can develop a new perspective for himself, as his existing attitudes to language may be a key element in preventing his effective use of language for learning. Moreover, Language Study should not stop at the provision of this perspective in relation only to *language for learning*. *Language for living* is an essential part of his ability to use language to learn. If we are going to be serious about attempting to meet '. . . the language needs of all children . . .', we cannot afford to stop at the class-room door.

I must now return to the main line of argument. To say that the development of an appropriate linguistic perspective is necessary for all those involved in the process of education is a very strong claim to make. What I want to do in this chapter is show how that claim arises not merely from the present situation in education, but out of the very way in which, as social beings, we are designed to use language. In order to do this I shall have to take a brief look at the process the sociologist refers to as 'socialization'. What this will show is that the climate affecting the use of language within the school or the college is created as much by the prevailing climate in the home and the community and society as a whole, as it is by the local conditions within the school itself or the educational system to which it belongs. Once I have done this, I will be in a position to go on and consider the way in which current changes in the educational system and in society affect the concept of Language Study.

One of the most necessary tasks for Language Study is to break down the idea that we can deal successfully with the problems of using language for learning by focusing solely upon the framework of the educational process itself. By looking at how a folk-linguistic perspective can shape an individual's view of language and its use, one can show that using language to learn is so bound up with using language to live that it does not make sense to treat them in isolation from one another. It also underlies the fact that every teacher needs to develop an *adequate* linguistic perspective in order to discover the effect of folk-linguistic perspective upon his attitudes to his own, and his pupils' use of language. In so far as we want to make sense of the language activity that goes on in schools and colleges, we must give up our habit of treating them as isolated autonomous institutions. The difference between viewing them as *institutions* and as *agencies* has already been referred to (see Chapter 1, Section 3, page 14). The next step is to relate this

20

distinction to the process of socialization, because it is this process that most intimately connects school and society through the medium of language. Schools and colleges as educational agencies stand in a special relationship to this process, moreover, which is why it is possible to refer to them as 'socializing agencies'. This is important from the point of view of Language Study, because language is one of the primary means by which *educational* agencies perform their function as *socializing* agencies.

To call schools and colleges agencies, then, is to express a particular theory about the part they play in the process by which individual men and women learn how to be effective members of society. Educational agencies play a dominant part in the pro-cess by which men acquire the particular '. . . capabilities and habits . . .' they need for survival in our society, as well as the values that bind them together as a society. A contemporary American linguist, whose chief interest is the relationship between language and culture, goes as far as to say that:

> . . . language itself is a social institution with the function of value integration.

I would prefer to say 'social agency', but the implications of the remark are clear enough. If we are interested in how men use language to live, we must face the fact that one of their chief uses for it is to give an individual identity to the multiplicity of social groups that go to make up a society, groups such as family, com-munity, office and workshop and school. This identity arises out of shared values and activities which are made available to the newcomer through the process of socialization. Unless we focus on this process, then, we are unlikely to make sense of the ways in which they use language to live, because we will not understand what values those ways are expressing.

Having said as much, it follows that the scope of Language Study must include a consideration of the wider contexts in which the teacher is operating. Certainly, the language activity within the learning situation itself, the pattern of language in use between teachers and pupils in class-rooms, must be at the very centre of its focus. At the same time, wherever the focus is upon the immedi-ate linguistic events involved in a particular pattern of class-room activity, we need to remember that that class-room exists in the social context of the school as a whole; and that that school exists in the context of a particular neighbourhood, in a particular community. Moreover, we must not forget that that school also

21

has a place as an educational agency within the larger context of a particular educational system. In its turn, this educational system exists within the even larger context provided by what we understand as 'society'. Similarly, the neighbourhood and community which provide the immediate social context for the school belong in their turn and in their own way to this same thing we call 'society'. Just to add a final level of complication to the whole picture, it is entirely proper to speak of family, school, neighbourhood and community as each possessing their own culture, and, at the same time partaking of the culture of the larger context to which they belong.

What I have tried to show in this section is that there is no sense in which we are entitled to say that our concern with language in teaching and learning may profitably stop at the boundaries of the class-room or the school. The more we focus upon the problems created in school by the '. . . language needs of all children . . .' the more we are forced to extend our horizons until they embrace the whole range of '. . . capabilities and habits . . .' which go to make up the culture of a society. This we must do, because our concern is with language and the use of language, and language is, as Edward Sapir once said:

> . . . a complex inventory of all the ideas, interests and occupations that take up the attention of the community.

2. Language for living and language for learning

The term language for living introduced in the last chapter may have made some readers uneasy. It might seem to suggest a too heavily emotional attitude towards the part played by language in the lives of men and their society. Nothing of the kind is intended, however. The phrase is offered as a simple descriptive label for the fact that men use language in some way or other throughout the whole spectrum of their activities as individuals and social beings. It does, however, imply a particular view of the nature and function of language, a view that regards language as the defining characteristic of man as a species and therefore as a crucial element in his ability to survive, individually and collectively. Professor Max Black, a philosopher whose central interest is the part played by language in our capacity to function as thinking animals, puts it this way,

> Man is the only animal that can talk . . . He alone can bridge

the gap between one person and another, conveying thoughts, feelings, desires, attitudes, and sharing in the traditions, conventions, the knowledge and the superstition of his culture . . . On this essential skill depends everything that we call civilisation. Without it, imagination, thought—even self-knowledge—are impossible.

What Professor Black says is obviously the case. The trouble is that it is *so obviously* the case that we are constantly being led to overlook its implications, because we live them out in every aspect of our lives, every day that we live. This very obviousness can become a serious liability when we are concerned with the question of the part played by language in education. As I have suggested elsewhere:

When something enters into every aspect of our lives in the way in which language does, its very familiarity is a barrier to exploration. Existing understanding will always seem sufficient, and exploration merely a process of elaborating an abstruse disguise for what is commonplace and familiar.

One major aim of Language Study is to show that it is precisely the commonplace and the familiar in our use of language for living which is most in need of exploration, if we are to understand how we use language to learn. We need to be able to create a climate of opinion in which no teacher would be willing to accept that his everyday familiarity with language, as a competent native speaker, was sufficient *in itself* to provide him, as a teacher, with what he needs to know about its nature and function.

If we now consider the second of our terms, language for learning, we can see that the pupil finds himself in a similar situation, because his competence as a native speaker will not *of itself* provide him with what he needs to know about language for learning. In other words, the understanding of the nature and function of language which we derive from our capacity to use it as competent native speakers does not make it easy for us to reflect upon our knowledge of the language, or our knowledge of the use of the language. We learn language in such a way that our knowledge of it, and of its use, are necessarily intuitive. We function successfully as users of language just because we do not need to deploy an explicit body of knowledge in so doing, as we do if we wish to function successfully as users of Physics, or Mathematics, or History, or Social Science. This distinction is a very important one, but its exploration in detail is not material to the argument

23

of this chapter. May I, therefore, refer the interested reader to Chapter Two of *Exploring Language* where I offer an analysis of what we should understand by 'knowledge OF a language'? In particular, I draw a basic distinction between 'knowledge OF a language' and 'knowledge ABOUT a language' in these terms:

> Knowledge OF a language derives solely from the process of learning language, while knowledge ABOUT language embraces the intuitions of folk-linguistic and all kinds of knowledge about that are conscious and explicit.

This distinction between 'knowledge OF a language' and 'knowledge ABOUT a language' is crucial to the idea of language for learning. When we want to focus upon the question of pupils' needs in the context of learning situations, we must be very clear about the kind of 'knowledge' that would be relevant. Pupils are competent speakers of a language because they have acquired a natural language in the process of growing up as ordinary members of a human community. It is this 'knowledge OF the language' which they bring with them into the class-room. It is *operational knowledge* of the language in the sense that it provides each pupil with a capacity to use language for living. This means that he is in a position to produce spoken utterance or written text in so far as he can *read* the situation in which he finds himself. His ability to read a situation and then draw upon his *operational knowledge* in order to meet its demands necessarily depends, therefore, upon his intuitive assessment of how he can use language to live. It follows from this that an individual's knowledge of his language can only become operational for him in so far as he is able to form an intuitive assessment of what using language might look like in a particular situation. Unless we are prepared to show pupils, therefore, what using language for learning really looks like, we must not be surprised if they are unable to deploy their knowledge of the language effectively to meet the linguistic demands of the learning situations in which we meet them.

An individual's knowledge of his language, therefore, becomes *operational* when he adds to his fundamental knowledge of the language a corresponding knowledge of the use of the language. We can speak of these two 'knowledges', then, as different aspects of an individual's *linguistic resource,* and together we can say that they provide him with his capacity. We possess a very strong intuition that this distinction is a real distinction and our sense of it has entered into a whole range of everyday expressions. Consider what we mean by 'words failed me', 'I was lost for words', 'I just didn't know what to say', 'I can't find words to express it', 'I was speechless', 'He hadn't a word to say for himself'. A common element in all these expressions is surely the sense that the 'words' *are* there, but we can't lay our tongues on them at that precise moment in that particular setting. What our intuition points to is the fact that we may indeed be aware that we possess relevant intuitive knowledge of the elements and structure of the language, but be quite unable to deploy them on occasions, because we seem to lack a correspondingly relevant intuitive knowledge of how they might be used.

There is, however, yet another factor to be considered in relation to language for learning; it is the pupils' folk-linguistic intuitions about language and the use of language. These intuitions constitute a third kind of 'knowledge', and influence our capacity to language effectively just as much as either of the other two. They are, however, knowledge ABOUT language rather than knowledge OF language, although, as will be seen, it is knowledge ABOUT of a rather special kind. Consider for a moment popular views about accent or dialect; about the relationship between spoken and written language; about correctness in speech or writing. Consider the fact that many people write and talk about language as though it were made up of 'words' only; that others regard their favoured form of the written language as the correct form, a form of which speech is but an imperfect copy; that others regard usage acquired from another language as necessarily a sign of linguistic decline. Think of the implications of phrases like 'Actions speak louder than words', 'What we want is action, not words', 'Mere talk', 'Don't bandy words with me', 'Don't answer back'. All of these express a particular view of how we use language to live and, even more importantly how some of us think how we all ought to use language to live.

What these views reveal are attitudes and assumptions about the nature and function of language which enter into a person's whole way of regarding the part language plays in his life. He has acquired them by growing up as a member of a particular social group within a particular human community. In that sense they are a product of cultural learning; they are intimately a part of the way in which he looks at the world. This idea can be tested by challenging the expression of such views. The reaction is likely to be very strongly felt. It is also likely to imply that the challenge must be unserious, because the views expressed are so *obvious* to the

25

holder that he can conceive of no other way of looking at the topic to which they refer. These views are intuitive, therefore, in the sense that they do shape a speaker's own use of language, and his response to how others use it, without his being continuously conscious of the fact. At the same time, however, they are knowledge ABOUT language rather than knowledge OF language, and consequently it is possible to create a situation in which people can be made aware of what their own folk-linguistic views might be. It is even possible to create situations in which they can go on to modify their folk-linguistic attitudes in the light of a new perspective on language.

In the final section of this chapter, I want to draw together this discussion of language for living and language for learning by suggesting how the different factors we have looked at come together to create a particular climate for language activity within the environment of school or college. In doing this, I hope I shall be able to show that the need for Language Study arises out of the very nature of language activity itself and its relationship to the environment we create for ourselves as social beings. If I am successful in this, then I will have shown that every teacher needs to be able to reflect upon his own and his pupils' use of language, because there is no teacher who does not contribute to the creation of the climate for language activity within which he and all his colleagues have to work. I will also have shown, moreover, that every teacher's attitudes and assumptions about language not only affect the local climate of opinion in the school, but also contribute powerfully to the attitudes and assumptions current within the larger context of community and society.

3. Language and cultural learning

In the first section of this chapter I spoke about the way in which men use language to create and maintain the individual identity of the human groups which go to make up the total organization of society. I pointed to the process the sociologist calls socialization as the primary means by which these groups are able to perpetuate themselves and suggested that language plays a crucial part in the process. I want to emphasize the fact that this process is concerned with the way in which newcomers to a group learn how to be members of it and that a crucial aspect of the whole business is their induction into the complex web of values, capabilities and habits which go to make up the life of that group. Alternatively,

26

we can say that socialization is the process of cultural learning by means of which a newcomer learns how to function adequately as a member of society. We can think of a child, therefore, as having *to learn his way into* the society to which he belongs by birth or by adoption.

As well as being a member of society, however, he also belongs to a family and a community. Each of these is an example of a *human group* and each socializes the child in two ways. From the point of view of society as a whole, it is through his membership of such *socializing agencies* as these that the child learns what values, capabilities and habits characterize the culture of the society in which he finds himself. Our own experience tells us, however, that some of the things which we learn through being socialized into our own family are not characteristic of families in general, but are unique to that one particular family. This is because a particular social group, whether a family, a school or a community, does have a pattern of values, capabilities and habits uniquely its own, and as we acquire the language of the group so we acquire these values, capabilities and habits which are peculiar to it. Whether we are focusing on the patterns of society as a whole or on those unique to particular social groups the most potent way in which values, capabilities and habits are acquired is through learning the language, because so many elements of the culture are embedded in the patterns of the language itself.

Being a member of a school is like being a member of any other human group in the sense that membership, whether for teacher or for pupil, necessarily involves the individual in a many-levelled process of cultural learning. At one level, schools and colleges act as socializing agencies in that they mediate the values, capabilities and habits characteristic of the culture of the society in which they occur, just like any other social group within that society. At another, they mediate the values, capabilities and habits which combine to give unique identity to a particular school or college. Unlike most other groups, however, schools and colleges also function on a third level as *educational* agencies. Their function is to pass on a quite specific set of values, capabilities and habits, the explicit operational skills like reading and writing, and the organized bodies of knowledge that a society believes it has need of. Moreover, this function is explicitly recognized in society and constitutes the public view of what they exist to do.

We are now in a position to relate the process of cultural learning to the distinction we have made between language for living and language for learning. In so far as the school or college functions as a *socializing agency*, language for living will have to be used *even in the learning situation itself*. How and where, and in what ways, we have been socialized determine how we use language to live. Consequently, the language for living that learners have available for entering into the social life of the school is a language shaped by their background and not by the school. On the other hand, language for learning only arises where the use of language arises out of the need to pass on operational skills and organized knowledge. Language for learning is, therefore, something that the school makes available through its own activities as an educational agency rather than a use of language which learners bring into the school with them from their life outside.

We can now link this to what was said earlier about folk-linguistic attitudes. If we ask the basic question—what *are* folk-linguistic attitudes?—one answer is to say that they represent a society's attitudes and assumptions about language and its use. As this is the case, they are the product of socialization, and as language is one of the major means by which socialization is accomplished, we will find that the process gives rise to attitudes and assumptions about language and its use wherever it operates. When we focus upon language activity within the school, then, we can expect to find a variety of different folk-linguistic attitudes and assumptions occurring side by side.

The school itself will produce perspectives in relation to its function as a social agency and as an educational agency, and there is no reason to suppose that these will be congruent. Teachers and pupils will each have their own perspective, as individuals standing in differing relationships to the cultural values of society as a whole and as members of different social groups, each with its own set of cultural values concerning language and its use. Moreover, these differences in perspective relate to language for learning as much as to language for living.

For this reason above all, I would argue that the point of departure for an effective approach to Language Study must be a consideration of the attitudes of teachers and pupils towards language; what they are, where they come from; what leads to their perpetuation and how they may be modified. I want to end by pointing to one further complicating factor. Language is not only the major means through which we gain possession of the values, capabilities and habits which go to make up our culture, but it is *itself* one of those capabilities, and its use involves the

28

learning of a whole set of linguistic values and habits. Hence, whenever we have to concern ourselves with patterns of language in use, whether for living or for learning, we will find ourselves forced to consider what it means to be socialized into a society, or a culture, or a particular variety of human group, and how the necessary process of cultural learning involves us also in a process of learning how to use language.

3 Language, learners and a changing society

1. Social diversity and its demands upon the individual

Up to this point, the argument for Language Study has been made in terms of the basic needs of teachers and learners. These needs have been shown to arise out of the very nature and function of language itself in its role as the primary medium for cultural learning. The heart of the problem is our need to use explicitly for educational ends within the school and college what we acquire and use intuitively for personal ends within the family and the community.

I want to turn now to the question of change, within the educational system and within society itself. I write from within a complex advanced industrial society, and I am likely to be read by many who live within societies that are very differently organized. I would suggest, however, that it is those elements in the organization of an advanced industrial society which most directly affect the use of language to live and language to learn that are appearing in newly industrialized societies throughout the world.

I want to show that the nature and direction of the changes taking place within society and within the educational system enormously reinforce the need for a linguistic perspective, whether we are considering the use of language for living or language for learning. This is an enormous topic and deserves a whole book to itself. All I can do in this context is to indicate the relevance of Language Study to some of the key problems which are likely to arise in a changing society, especially those problems which are likely to arise in an emergent society when an advanced industrial society is taken as a model for change. Such problems can be seen in terms of patterns of change, their diversity, tempo and cumulative effect upon the life-histories of individual human beings.

Perhaps the most obvious difference between the world one's pupils live in and the world their great-grand parents lived in as children is the sheer diversity of function and focus it now contains. The majority of our pupils are urban dwellers. They grow up in the social context of an enormously complex network of relationships, stretching from the intimate circle of the nuclear family, through the circle of the neighbourhood, peer group and the school, to all the contacts that they make with other human beings in the course of using the facilities and services of their community. They may find themselves moving from one community to another in the course of their father's need to follow job opportunities. What they do when they leave school is a matter of choice. In order to find the job they want, or even any job at all, they may have to go on their travels, live a life independent of neighbourhood ties, come into contact with parts of the country quite different from any they have ever met before. In many parts of Europe, this diversity of situation has already come to include other countries and this could easily become the case for those now at school in Britain.

The diversity of focus in our society shows clearly when we observe the large groups within it who develop and maintain their own view of the world. Each group expresses its uniqueness through a particular pattern of values, capabilities and habits. Where we find this diversity we can properly speak of a *plural* society. Looking at these varied patterns it becomes increasingly difficult to talk in terms of a single *unitary* culture, the values of which will be recognized and accepted by all those who happen to speak the same mother tongue. In such a situation, it also becomes increasingly difficult to maintain the fiction that there is, or ought to be, congruence between the values, attitudes and assumptions of any one group dominant in a society and the very different values, attitudes and assumptions to be found in other parts of it. The maintenance of such a fiction, however, is of particular relevance to relationships in schools and colleges, for if the fiction is maintained then there will be the assumption that, they, the schools and colleges, must as educational agencies, mediate the values of this one group. If this happens, then a credibility gap will open between the view of the world which the educational system takes as axiomatic and the view of the world that governs the lives of the majority of the learners it is supposed to serve. This is the situation which we are now faced with in Britain.

From what was said in the previous chapter about the role of socialization in integrating our collective activities as human beings, it follows that a key feature of cultural diversity is a corresponding linguistic diversity. The linguistic diversity that matters in the context of a plural society, however, is that which expresses fundamental attitudes and assumptions about the world. For example, we are all familiar with the way in which the sound patterns of a language can show diversity in terms of accent and dialect. This, however, is much more a matter of *locality* than attitude. In these terms, the phonological diversity in the way in which working class pupils from Newcastle or Liverpool or Birmingham form the sounds of the language is far less important than the congruence that exists is their use of language to live, and in their assumptions about using language to learn. Cultural diversity generates linguistic diversity in such a way that teachers and learners are very likely to find themselves repeatedly at cross-purposes, because each assumes that their way of using language is the only way of using language, whether for living or learning. In such a situation, surely we need to be able to stand outside our culture-bound use of the language in order to see how others use it? In the context of the learning situation, it is at least arguable that teachers should take the lead in this activity and this they can only do by developing an appropriate linguistic perspective.

From the learner's point of view, however, an equally important aspect of this diversity is more social than cultural, because it is concerned with interpersonal relations rather than with underlying attitudes and assumptions about the world. It can best be expressed in terms of the multiplicity of roles that the individual now has to assume in the course of his life as an ordinary member of society. There is one pattern of relationships centred on the home, another on work, another on leisure, another involving contact with public agencies, and so on, with very little overlap between them. The following quotation suggests why these relationships are so important from a Language Study point of view:

> Who people are, what they do together, and for what purpose they do it, provides a mesh which yields the picture of a pattern of relationship or a pattern of language, depending on the angle of one's vision.

An individual who has to enter into a very large number of relationships of many different kinds will have a much greater need for a wide variety of ways of speaking than one who lives out his life within the limits of a very small network of relationships. In fact, we can say that the more diverse a man's range of activities, the more diverse the kind and condition of the other people with whom he comes in contact, the greater will be the demand he has to make upon his command of the language in order to survive. We can say, therefore, that survival in such circumstances will depend ultimately upon a man's understanding of the enormous variety of different ways in which people can use language for living within the confines of the society.

If we accept the validity of this position, then we must accept that the development of the necessary operational competence to meet the linguistic demands of an indefinately variable pattern of social relationships is a key '. . . language need' for anyone who has to live in our kind of society. It follows that the development of this competence must be a major objective for our educational system, and therefore properly a feature of every teacher's professional concerns so far as they have responsibility for pupils' use of language. This responsibility, moreover, extends to language for living as well as language for learning, because the life of a school is social as well as educational. In order to meet it teachers need to know what is involved. They need an adequate account of the part played by language in sustaining the fabric of a complex society, social and linguistic, and they need to see how this account could then be related to practical class-room activities designed to bring about the development of the competence that is called for. A Language Study approach ought to take the responsibility for helping the teacher with both these tasks. A first attempt to provide the necessary account of language, relationships and society will be found in chapters five and six of *Exploring Language,* while *Language in Use* offers a concrete example of how this can be worked out in terms of practical class-room activities.

2. The demands of a changing society

If we now turn to consider the *tempo* of change in our society, we find a similarly disturbing situation. This is a feature of our world that is much spoken about and there is little need to detail its characteristics, but perhaps the very familiarity of the idea has blunted our perception of some of the most significant consequences that follow from it. Let me put it in terms of an individual's expectations, his ideas about the sort of world he is going to live in and what he is going to do to make a living for himself and his

33

family. In 1900, a man aged 20 would have believed that the future was going to be very little different from the past. He would do one job for his working life, do it in one town, probably even in one firm. The town was likely to be the town of his birth, the job the same as his fathers. In 1925, a young man of 20 would probably have believed much the same. In 1950, a young man would be much more likely to see himself making moves of one kind or other, changing jobs or changing firms or changing towns. He would still see these moves as major decisions, however, and unlikely to occur more than once or twice in his working life. That he would have been wrong is a measure of the degree to which significant changes in the structure and organization of a society do not always impinge immediately upon the consciousness of those they are going to affect most directly.

If we come now to the present generation in our schools and colleges, the very least that we can say is that the world in which they celebrate their 65th birthday, the world of the 2020ies, will be even more unlike our own world than our own world is unlike the world of 1900. What has happened in this century is that the rate of change has increased out of all proportion to anything men have known in earlier periods. It has reached a point where change grows upon itself, so that we are creating a society in which the *normal* state of that society is one of change. This goes against some of our deepest assumptions, because the way we look at change is a product of our cultural learning and our view of it is expressed through terms which imply the desirability of staying where one is, unless a move is really necessary. Our whole way of speaking about change assumes that what we mean by it is a move from a present position to a future position; each position, the old and the new, is a position of stability and what happens in between is a period of uncertainty which ought properly to be limited in scale and direction. A good example of this is provided by current attitudes to changes in the curriculum. Those who accept change as necessary assume that what curriculum development means is the replacement of the old set of subject contents and received patterns of work by a new set. Once that has been worked out then curriculum change ceases. Hostility occurs where teachers sense that what these present changes point towards is a situation in which there will be no new set to replace the old, only a programme for continuous change.

Their hostility is not surprising when everything in our educational tradition reinforces the idea that change is perhaps neces-

34

sary, but only as a device for moving from one fixed order to another. For instance, school is still run on the assumption that what you learn there is not only relevant to your needs in adult life immediately on leaving school, but will remain indefinitely relevant throughout adult life because that adult life will remain more or less the same. What I have said about the tempo of change in our society, however, argues a widening credibility between the view of the world our educational system offers and what is actually happening. This situation has produced the tensions which underlie the present call for *relevance* in rethinking the curriculum. The system as it is at present does not begin to meet the needs of learners, now that they face a society in a process of continuous change. One of the best attempts to look at the problem in educational terms is called *Teaching as a subversive activity*. In it Neil Postman and Charles Weingartner sum up the effects of the tempo of change by saying that:

> we have reached the stage where change occurs so rapidly that each of us in the course of our lives has continuously to work out a set of values, beliefs, and patterns of behaviour that are viable, or *seem* viable, to each of us personally. And just when we have identified a workable system, it turns out to be irrelevant because so much has changed while we were doing it.

The cumulative effect upon the individual human being is to place an enormous emphasis upon his powers of adaption. Man is a problem-solving animal and his capacity to survive is bound up with his capacity to deal with the heuristic in his life. Working out what it means to be a problem-solving animal was the central concern of the psychologist George Kelly. His theory of personal constructs is very relevant to the present argument, because it enables me to show how my reference to Postman and Weingartner on the impact of continuous change relates to the current need for a Language Study approach.

Summarizing Kelly's fundamental postulate, Bannister and Fransella suggest that:

> . . . a man checks how much sense he has made of the world by seeing how well his 'sense' enables him to anticipate it.

Kelly stresses that:

> man is in business to make sense out of his world and to test the sense he has made in terms of its predictive capacity.

If the preceding arguments about the diversity and the tempo

35

of change are accepted, then the least we can say is that the task of making sense out of the world, and using the results as a basis for predicting what is going to happen next, will be extremely complicated by the kind of society in which change is continuous. Making sense of things while standing still may be difficult enough in itself, but we have now created a world which everyone is expected to make sense of while standing on a moving stairway. If human beings are in business to produce 'predictive capacity', as Kelly suggests, then a changing society will make his task progressively more taxing. The diversity and tempo of change renders obsolete the sense we make of our world even as we make it.

So we have a situation in which the most important single need for survival becomes the individual's ability to revise continuously the sense he makes of his world because that world is changing continuously, and his effective 'predictive capacity' rests upon the sense that he makes of it. It is reasonable to argue, therefore, that success in developing and operating a 'predictive capacity' will be very closely linked to an individual's success in developing an operational command over spoken and written language. If we remember the part played by language in cultural learning, we can see that, whatever else may be necessary in this situation, human beings must be able to review the part played by language in shaping their view of the world. The ability to 'work out a set of values, beliefs, and patterns of behaviour' is, after all, dependent upon our capacity to language. The linguistic form we give to what we learn through the process of socialization, moreover, is often decisive in determining our view of the world. Altering that view of the world, therefore, will depend upon the degree to which we can draw upon our capacity to language for a range of alternative linguistic forms that will give us alternative ways of looking at the world. It follows then, that another essential aspect of meeting '. . . the language needs of all children' is the creation of a learning environment in which they can come to appreciate how language is used to embody *alternative views of reality*.

3. The effects of change on school and curriculum

In the preceding sections of this chapter, I focused upon the idea of change and the way it now affects the life and organization of society, in order to show that it has created a climate which makes exceptionally heavy demands upon any individual's ability to use language for living. Given the nature of the relationship between

36

society and school a change in the one is certain to bring about parallel changes in the environment for learning provided by the other. This section, therefore, explores the nature of these changes, and looks at the implications for the use of *language for learning*, because change creates new situations, new situations create new patterns of relationship and new relationships demand new ways of speaking for their effective realization. The eventual success or otherwise of these changes in the environment of school and college, therefore, will depend upon the degree to which teachers and learners are willing and able to rethink their use of language for teaching and for learning.

I want to refer once more to the York Conference from which I took my key quotation for Chapter 1. In his own summing up of the work of the conference Professor Wayne Booth of Chicago University set out to place the activities of the conference in the broader context of the current educational scene as a whole. In particular he suggested that the conference represented the efforts of one large group of teachers within the educational system to come to terms with a radically new concept of the child. This he described in the following way:

the child is an inherently curious, inherently purposive creature, a creature whose thoughts will be passion-ridden and whose feelings are bound with cognitions, a creature made for and by symbol exchange, a creature made in and through the language which by his own irrepressible needs he helps to create.

Although Professor Wayne Booth refers explicitly to *the child*, I want the reader to see that this is really a radically new way of looking at individual human beings, whatever their age. It seems unlikely that so fundamental a form of behaviour would only operate in the earliest years of life. What Professor Wayne Booth says about the child, therefore, can be taken to apply as much to students as to pupils and as much to teachers as to learners.

Professor Wayne Booth is really advancing four propositions about the nature and function of man:

1) '. . . the child is an inherently curious, inherently purposive creature . . .'

To say that he is *inherently* curious and purposive is in accord with Kelly's view of man as a problem-solving animal. This heuristic bias is a product of man's genetic design and therefore must have great survival value for the species. What this suggests is that there is a very powerful drive built into the make up of every human being which compels him to make sense of his world. If he finds that he is unable to do so, however hard he tries, or sees that he is being prevented from doing so, the result will be an enormous sense of frustration.

This proposition can be related to the current educational scene in two quite distinct ways. The pressure towards a more child-centred learning situation, and the idea of the learner as one who should be asked to solve real problems rather than commit to memory other people's solutions, derive from this view of the child as a person who is *designed* to be curious and purposive. On the other hand, it can be suggested that hostility and apathy towards school and college have their origin as much in the frustrating of this basic need to make sense of the world as in anything else. The knowledge we now have about the effects of stress upon the individual indicate that there are two basic responses available, hysteria and apathy. One leads to hostility and ultimately to expressive violence, the other to disinterest and ultimately to withdrawal. From a linguistic point of view, if we try to bring about learning situations that satisfy the needs of learners as problem-solving animals we cannot avoid creating quite new demands upon their use of language for learning. At the same time, hostility and apathy may well arise if pupils are unable to use the language for learning that their teacher demands. It is often the case that no one has tried to make this language for learning available to them, or considered its relevance to their needs in the particular learning situation concerned. In either case, one part of a successful approach to the problem is likely to include a sharp focus upon the patterns of language used in the learning situations, and that focus a linguistic view of language can provide.

2) '. . . a creature whose thoughts will be passion-ridden and whose feelings are bound with cognitions . . .'

If it is true that man is a creature whose 'thoughts will be passion-ridden and whose feelings are bound with cognitions', then a major challenge is presented to the curriculum as we know it. Much of our professional thinking is based upon the implicit assumption that there is a fundamental dichotomy between thought and feeling; that we can happily plan a curriculum which pursues affective and cognitive goals in separation from each other.

I would suggest that the insights contained in this particular proposition underlie a great many of the current efforts at changing

38

the curriculum, such as the development of a new perspective in science teaching, especially the life sciences; in the work towards a new concept of the humanities; and, in this country, in the programmes suggested for those who will now be remaining at school beyond fifteen. I would suggest, also, that it accounts in part for the impetus towards the widespread use of a thematic approach and for the urge to develop effective methods of team teaching.

Once again, there are two distinct ways in which these changes in the curriculum affect the use of language for learning. Firstly, they alter the patterns of relationship within the learning situation, and in the social and cultural life of the school or the college as a whole; and, secondly, they put a premium upon the ability of teachers and learners to find new ways of speaking which will fit these new ways of relating to each other as teachers and learners. In so far as these changes reflect a shift away from the old dichotomy between thought and feeling, however, they create a demand for new varieties of language for learning, because the terms and phrases which provide the patterns for existing *varieties* have this distinction built into them. This is because the technical language we use for the subjects we teach is not only a form of descriptive language, but also a way of recording a particular view of the world. Should that view of the world change in any fundamental way, as it surely must if we accept this new relationship between thought and feeling, then we can only express our sense of the change by modifying the language we have been accustomed to use for the discussion of particular areas of knowledge.

Modifying language habits of this kind usually requires us to modify, in turn, our views of what we want language to do for us in relation to a particular area of operations like the teaching of a curriculum subject. This situation of change, therefore, makes great demands upon our ability to review the whole range of our professional attitudes towards language for learning. Reviewing 'the tools for the trade', however, implies flexibility towards our own choice of language in the learning situation. This is only attainable in so far as we are prepared to develop an adequate linguistic perspective, but even if we are fully prepared to consider the questions involved we cannot do so successfully, without an appropriate form of Language Study to draw upon.

Between the third and fourth propositions we are considering there is a special relationship, in that the most potent system of symbols available to man is the language that he speaks.

3) '. . . a creature made for and by symbol-exchange . . .'

The idea that man is a creature made for and by symbol-exchange is really saying something about the fundamental relationship between the individual and the world he inhabits. It is suggesting that we have to translate our experience of the world into a pattern of symbols before we can be said to 'know' what we have expressed. We are *made for* this process, in the sense that our brains are designed to operate in this way, and we are *made by* it, in so far as we know what we can symbolize, and what we know about the world makes us what we are. As Kelly says 'a particular man *is* the sense he makes of the world'. So far, so good, but unless we can share what we know through an *exchange of symbols*, we have no means of testing the general validity of what we know, and, as Kelly suggests, we are in business to test the validity of our predictions about the world. If we want to see what happens to our knowledge of the world when we cannot test it through an exchange of symbols, we have only to look at the plight of the autistic child or the paranoic.

How then does so abstract an idea relate to the climate of change in the class-room? I suggest that this proposition underlines the importance of our ability to make sense of the world, and of the fact that human beings have a *biological* need to interpret new experience successfully, if they are to maintain their capacity to function as individual sentient selves. The corollary of this is that if they cannot make meaning out of new experiences satisfactory to themselves, they suffer distress which, repeated frequently, leads in the end to a complete breakdown in their ability to relate to the world.

If we have a climate of continuous change in society, then the struggle to make meanings out of a continuous flux of new experience demands an ability to perform rapidly and successfully a whole range of symbol-exchanges. It would be proper to argue that schools and colleges are in business to facilitate symbol-exchange, and that they have a special responsibility in this direction. However, when we remember that the climate of change in society brings about a similar climate in schools and colleges we see that schools and colleges have to cope with the learner's needs both as an individual in a rapidly changing world *and* as a learner in a rapidly changing educational system. After all that has been said so far, it is not surprising that the attitudes of the school, the teacher and the learner, towards language play a decisive part in the success or failure of any attempts to meet this dual need.

40

Indeed, the fourth proposition we have to consider suggests that it could hardly do otherwise.

4) 'A creature made in and through the language which by his own irrepressible needs he helps to create . . .'

This proposition presents one special instance of the operation of symbol-exchange, the human use of language to create meaning out of experience. It underlines the point that language is so intimately a part of us that our view of the world is inseparable from the way we use language to shape it. It also stresses that our own individual identity, and *our knowledge of that identity*, is a product of the activity of using language to live. Finally, it points to the fact that that language which we use for these purposes is not only 'out there', a thing wholly public and external to our functioning as individual human beings, but also 'in here', a thing so intimately ours that we can create unique meanings with its aid.

In one sense, there is little more to say. As language plays so central a part in the autonomy and operational effectiveness of individual human beings, then their capacity for survival is seriously affected, in so far as they find themselves continuously in a situation where their attempts to make sense of new experience is frustrated by their lack of the necessary language for learning or language for living.

Our failure to consider sufficiently carefully *the linguistic demands* that arise from a pattern of change in the curriculum is in the process of creating precisely such a situation in our schools and colleges.

4 Language Study: discipline or process?

1. Relevant considerations

In the last chapter, I suggested that the diversity and tempo of change in our society have brought about a situation in which the individual is increasingly at risk, unless he can respond rapidly and flexibly to continuously varying circumstances, personal, social and cultural. As our ability to make sense of the world and to make relationships with others depends ultimately upon our command of a language, the more demanding and complex the network of relationships we enter into the greater will be the cumulative strain upon our capacity to language. I also suggested that a similar situation has arisen within schools and colleges owing to the special relationship that exists between an educational agency and the society it serves. It is this dual climate of change as it affects the problems and processes of teaching and learning that provides the immediate context for Language Study.

Cumulatively, the three preceding chapters have argued the case for a new approach to the educational study of language in terms of the radical nature of the society men have created in this century and the fundamental nature of their use of language to live and to learn. I must now offer a design for such an approach that could be realized in terms of actual programmes of study in particular schools and colleges.

There are many respects in which this design for Language Study runs counter to the customary ways of thinking about new areas of interest within the educational system or establishing a new subject in the curriculum. I do not think there is any point in talking about Language Study as though it were but one more subject to add to the list for an already overcrowded curriculum, and I would not accept the addition of an element of academic

Linguistic Science to the curriculum of teacher education as an adequate answer to the need for a Language Study approach in that context. The difficulty lies in our need to focus upon patterns of language for living and language for learning, because these are patterns of language *in use* and language in use constitutes a unique focus for enquiry, owing to the way in which we learn how to use language, what we learn along with it, and what we do with it when we have learnt it.

I have focused attention upon the fact that man is a problem-solving animal whose integrity as an individual sentient self depends upon his continuing ability to make sense of his world and to form relationships with other similarly individual sentient selves. His ability to do either of these things is profoundly affected by his capacity to language. Values, capabilities and habits are transmitted through language, moreover, and it is these values, capabilities and habits, which guide him in his interpretation of the world and his relationship with others, because they provide him with his only models for judging what is and is not the case. Language plays a vital part, therefore, in the whole process of cultural learning but it is itself a product of the same process, and therein lies its uniqueness as a focus of enquiry and the heart of the problem for the educational study of language.

> The uniqueness of language derives from the fact that it is, at one and the same time, a capability man acquires through growing up as a member of a particular society and the major means by which he can acquire all the other capabilities . . .

that go to make up the personal, social and cultural life of a particular family, community and society. This is to say that, at any one time, a man's capacity to language is the product of a particular way of life, led in a particular community, at a particular time, and has built into it, therefore, one particular set of personal, social and cultural values. They form the basis of his reading of the world, but they have themselves been shaped in his mind by the very language through which he gained access to them.

So we are faced with the inescapable fact that man's major means for making sense of his world has built into its elements and structure a bias towards interpreting experience in terms of a pre-existing set of categories, attitudes and assumptions. Should he live in a world subject to continuous social and cultural change, therefore, this bias must act as a continuous check upon his

43

attempts to make sense of the new, because it will always make it easier for him to language the new in terms of what he found appropriate for languaging the old. There are many who would say that there is nothing we can do about this, because it is simply 'human nature'. 'Human nature', however, is as much a construct as any other concept we use to make sense of the world, and the way we language the concept plays a vital part in our understanding of what we mean by it. Does this not suggest, therefore, that, if we were more adept at seeing how our language shapes the concepts we use, we might find less difficulty in modifying the constructs that go to make them? This implies that the development of a capacity *to reflect upon the part language plays in shaping our view of the world* is a vital part of everyone's equipment for survival in the sort of world we are already living in.

As educators, then, we must say that we cannot afford the comforting pessimism of an unchangeable 'human nature', but are bound to look for ways in which we can help all those we teach to cope with the world in which they have to live. A major priority must be the creation of conditions in which pupils can develop that ability to reflect upon the part language plays in their lives. It is an ability to stand back from the language we use in order to see how and why and in what ways that language mediates between us and our understanding of the world. The development of such an ability rests upon the growth of a *linguistic perspective* and it is for this reason that I would place the idea of linguistic perspective at the very centre of our professional concern with language. The nature and function of a linguistic perspective, where it comes from and how it operates, and what conditions are necessary for encouraging its development in teachers as well as in learners, therefore, provide the central focus for Language Study; whatever we put forward in relation to its design must be judged according to its value in forwarding this aim.

2. Disciplines, perspectives and reflexiveness

Linguistics is still a comparatively unfamiliar discipline, but this is not the place for me to give a detailed account of its structure and objectives. All I need to do is to show how its status as a discipline affects its relationship to Language Study. As I understand it, a discipline is a term for a particular way of looking at the world. If we take the standpoint of the biologist, the psychologist, the geographer or the economist, we view the world through his eyes,

44

which means that we use a particular set of concepts in our interpretation of it and use a particular pattern of language when we speak about it. What we are doing is to accept a particular perspective upon the world, biological, psychological, geographical or economistic. The most characteristic feature of these perspectives is the kind of question they encourage us to ask about the world, and it is commonplace that the questions we ask will determine the kind of evidence we look for, and, consequently, the kind of answers we get.

Let me illustrate this by showing how these four disciplines approach the study of man. Each asks its own questions about man: how does he function as a living organism? how does he function as a thinking being? how is he related to his environment? and how does he organize himself to supply his needs? The intellectual tradition we inherit from the nineteenth century stresses the autonomy of disciplines, the degree to which they exist in order to ask questions the answers to which are of unique interest to the disciplines themselves. Progressively through this century, however, people have become more and more aware of the relevance of the answers one discipline gives to its own questions to the questions which it is necessary to ask in a different field. To give an example which is illustrated by a book in this series: what biologists discover about the structure and function of the brain is highly relevant to what psychologists might have to say about man's cognitive activity. Putting this in terms of *perspective*, we can say that each discipline encourages the development and use of a particular way of looking at some aspect of the world, but that we are now increasingly aware of the limitations imposed upon our way of looking at things if we adopt the standpoint of a single perspective only. Especially is this the case if the focus of our interest is a complex phenomenon, like man, or his culture, or his society, or his language.

If we now consider the relationship between *linguistic* perspective and Linguistic Science, we will find an ambiguity similar to that which arose in the discussion of the educational use of the word 'need'. There is a proper sense in which we can refer to the particular way of looking at language which derives from the discipline of Linguistics as a 'linguistic perspective'. At the same time, however, it remains a most convenient term to use for man's ability to stand back from his habitual way of looking at language and its use. In the narrow sense, then, linguistic perspective is the linguist's characteristic way of viewing his subject matter: in the broad sense, it is the way in which a 'creature made in and through language . . .' learns to look at what has made him. Using the same term reminds us constantly that we cannot achieve a linguistic perspective on how we use language to live, unless we are prepared to make use of the linguistic perspective the linguist develops in the course of his own particular enquiries. At the same time, it should warn us that that perspective cannot tell us all we want to know, because it derives from one particular area of enquiry into language, and language is so complex a phenomenon in the life of man that no one discipline can ask all the necessary questions, and therefore no one discipline will provide all the answers.

What Language Study is interested in, therefore, is this *broad* sense of linguistic perspective, and the way in which it relates to our folk-linguistic perspective, the product of our habitual way of viewing the nature of function of language, which we operate intuitively, and which provides the basis for our everyday attitudes and assumptions concerning language and its use. What Language Study has to develop, therefore, is a perspective that is properly *reflexive* in the sense in which the social psychologist G. H. Mead used the word. In his theory, this term describes the relationship which arises when,

> . . . the individual's adjustment to the social processes is modified and refined by the awareness or consciousness which he thus has of it. It is by means of *reflexiveness*—the turning back of the experience of the individual upon himself—that the whole social process is thus brought into the experience of the individuals involved in it; it is by such means, which enable the individual to take the attitude of the other towards himself, that the individual is able consciously to adjust himself to that process. . . .

When I referred to the idea of the individual standing back from his habitual way of looking at language, in Mead's terms, I was suggesting that he should acquire the ability to 'turn back' upon himself his cumulative experience of languaging. In so far as the development of a linguistic perspective enables us to see how our capacity to language is primarily a product of a particular place, a particular time and a particular culture, it enables us '. . . to take the attitude of the other . . .', as far as language activity is concerned, because it makes us see that a view of the world is the product of an habitual way of using language, and is, by definition, particular and not universal.

46

3. Linguistics and Language Study

Let me now return to the relation between Linguistics and Language Study. I have laid stress upon the prominent role that we need to give to the identification and modification of attitudes and assumptions towards language, in developing a design for language study. We need to be free, therefore, to make use of the answers the linguist gives to his questions about the nature and function of language, in order to answer our own questions about the educational use of language. I have already given an account of how I see this relationship in Chapter Two, section 4, of *Exploring Language*, where I suggested that:

> Language Study, then, takes the needs of teachers and pupils as its criterion of relevance for selecting particular topics for exploration out of the whole range of Linguistic Studies. It recognises that teachers are interested in two kinds of knowledge about language, what will help them to understand the part played by language in the processes of learning and teaching and what will best show them how this part can be related to language as a feature of living, individual and social.

Language Study, therefore, will only be interested in using the work of academic Linguistic Studies in so far as that work can be related to the particular problems of language in teaching and learning. The primary need to modify the folk-linguistic perspective of teachers and learners, moreover, and encourage the development of a linguistic perspective that is properly reflexive, provides us with powerful criteria for selection and presentation. We cannot afford to make use of the findings of academic Linguistics, just because they are there; nor can we use findings, however relevant to the needs of teachers and learners, unless we can show how they relate to what goes on in actual learning situations.

We need to remember the hard truth we have all experienced in our own class-rooms that a knowledge of the facts does not automatically produce a change of attitude. 'Don't confuse me with facts, I've made up my mind', is a familiar enough saying from the world of public affairs, but it is no less common an occurrence in the world of education. When we are handling something as intimate and value-laden as language, where everyone regards his own view as authoritative, the chance of eliciting this response to an alternative view of the facts is quite extraordinarily high. An individual's feelings towards his own view of language, moreover, are often so strong that he will regard the presentation of an alternative view as a personal attack upon his integrity. Where his own view is expressed through the common language, and appears to be sanctioned by the very fact that the language itself provides familiar words and phrases for it, and where the alternative view must make use of a system of thought and a technical language which are quite unfamiliar, an explosive reaction is very likely, unless this state of affairs has been taken into account at the design stage. It is a common-place that such a reaction, should it occur, merely serves to reinforce a person's original view of the facts, and makes it that much more difficult to win a sympathetic hearing for a new approach. In this situation, encouraging teachers and learners to move towards a linguistic perspective must be a precondition for any extended exploration of language. In so doing, we must remember that the possession of a linguistic perspective on language is not the same thing as knowing what the discipline of Linguistics might have to say about the elements and structure of one's own, or any other, language.

We must now ask what kind of a perspective on language linguists can offer us. They hold differing views about the status of their subject, however, and some of these views are more helpful than others in relation to the concept of Language Study. We start with the common ground that Linguistics is a discipline asking its own questions about an aspect of the world and offering a body of knowledge about it that is rational and ordered. Some would say that a linguistic view is *an*, or even *the*, 'objective' view of the nature and function of language. This is not the place to go into the current debate about whether or not scientific enquiry is 'objective', in the popular sense of the word, but language is so intimate a function of being human that the problems of being a truly 'disinterested observer' are particularly acute, when language is the subject of our explorations. The position has been put most sharply by Professor Michael Polanyi,

> . . . as human beings, we must inevitably see the universe from a centre lying within ourselves and speak about it in terms of a human language shaped by exigencies of human intercourse. *Any attempt rigorously to eliminate our human perspective from our picture of the world must lead to absurdity.* (My italics)

If we need to use the work of a number of disciplines in order to develop a theory of language by means of which individual teachers and learners can develop a *linguistic* perspective, then the

48

last thing we can afford to do is to assume that, whilst teachers and learners have a *human* perspective, of which their view of language is a part, the disciplines themselves do not possess such a perspective, because they are 'objective'.

This point is important, because it is related to a basic division of opinion amongst linguists about what their field of enquiry and mode of operation should be. I shall simplify the position by suggesting that there are two views of the case current at the present time, the narrow and the broad. As in all such distinctions, the two views are here made to seem much more sharply defined than they actually appear in the work of any one linguist, but this simplification will show clearly where the problem lies for the development of a design for Language Study.

What I am calling the narrow view sees Linguistics as a discipline which is concerned exclusively with the organization of the sound patterns of natural languages, and their relationship to the corresponding organization of the internal pattern of those languages, phonological, grammatical and lexical. Those who hold to this point of view tend to believe that the Natural Sciences, especially 'hard data' sciences like Physics and Chemistry, provide the most appropriate models for their enquiries and for the criteria by which the results of those enquiries should be assessed. There is no doubt that this belief has produced most valuable results in certain fields, particularly those concerned with the production and reception of speech, the various branches of Phonetics. It has also produced an enormous body of descriptive information about the grammar and phonology of the world's natural languages. In particular, it has led to the development of a very powerful methodology for recording and analysing the patterns of languages which exists only as spoken languages. In terms of the actual number of different languages involved they constitute a far larger body then those which do make use of a writing system.

The total result has not been altogether happy, however, for two closely related reasons. Linguists have frequently adopted a view of what it is to practise science that does not bear very much relation to how scientists actually work. In particular, they have sought to use what they have understood by 'scientific method', and, in the process, they have set on one side many aspects of language in use, because these were too 'messy' to be accommodated within the terms of the rigorous system of enquiry that they chose to employ. The result has been a certain trivializing of the content of their enquiries in order to preserve the integrity of

49

the methodology they have adopted. In effect, the version of 'science' that informs their thinking would not be readily acceptable to those comtemporary scientists who have tried hardest to understand what it is to practise science. One of the most lucid and articulate is the distinguished British medical scientist, Sir Peter Medawar. Reviewing a recent book on this theme, Dr. Alex Comfort suggested that:

> For Medawar, science is an exercise in critical integrity operating on the fruits of the imagination. Without the imagination, no discovery: without the integrity of self-criticism, stratospheric hokum.

He might have gone on to say that enquiry without imagination, linked to a belief in a methodology that explicitly excludes the observer, leads to monumental irrelevance.

This is so important a question for the design of an approach to Language Study that I want to add to the discussion a key passage from Medawar's own writings. It is taken from the conclusion to his three lectures on *Induction and Intuition in Scientific Thought*:

> The purpose of scientific enquiry is not to compile an inventory of factual information, nor to build up a totalitarian world picture of natural Laws in which every event that is not compulsory is forbidden. We should think of it rather as a logically articulated structure of justifiable beliefs about nature. It begins as a story about a Possible World—a story which we invent and criticise and modify as we go along, so that it ends by being, as nearly as we can make it, a story about real life.

In the terms of my argument, '. . . a logically articulated structure of justifiable beliefs about . . .' language is what I would understand by a linguistic perspective, but ultimately this structure of beliefs has to be 'a story about real life', and a linguistic story that did justice to real life would have to tell the tale in terms of how people use language to live.

The narrow view of Linguistics tends to be accompanied by a strongly institutional view of the domain and function of the discipline and makes much use of dichotomies like 'theoretical' and 'practical', 'pure' and 'applied', 'linguistic' and 'non-linguistic'. In one sense, this is only to be expected in a young discipline, because our educational and academic system puts a premium upon the autonomy of the discipline, and is only prepared to tolerate a newcomer so long as it can show exclusive right to a field of enquiry. The controversy in this country over the

50

'right' of sociology to exist as an autonomous field of enquiry is only the most recent of many examples. Some readers may remember the similar controversy that surrounded the attempt to establish 'English' as a discipline, a controversy that can still erupt in the form of a challenge to the English Department to show what its 'content' is, what it actually 'teaches'. Unfortunately, an institutional view of linguistics is very hostile to the idea of 'using' linguistics in the ways which are necessary for a Language Study approach.

4. Language Study as a human science

Turning now to the broad view of Linguistic Science, I would suggest that it sees Linguistics as a *human* or *social* rather than a *natural* science. It is concerned with language as human behaviour, with language as 'the nervous system of our society', and as the medium through which we maintain a 'network of bonds and obligations'. These phrases are taken from *The Tongues of Men* by the late Professor Firth, a key figure for the idea of Linguistics as a human science. Elsewhere he has provided the most succinct definition of the broad view of linguistics that I have ever come across. When asked to define Linguistics, he said that 'the object of linguistic analysis is to make statements of meaning so that we can see how we use language to live'. This proposition implies that we should see linguistics associated with those disciplines which exist to pursue 'the proper study of man', especially Psychology and Sociology, the study of individual and social man respectively. As man makes himself a self in and through the language he speaks, and as he creates a society by using language to form a network of relationships with others, it is reasonable to suggest that the study of man as an individuating animal, and the study of man as a social animal, should be joined by the study of man as a talking animal, to form a triumvirate at the centre of our endeavour to understand ourselves.

What this view implies is the idea of a discipline as an *agency* rather than an institution. From this point of view, a discipline in the field of human science would be expected to show an openness towards other fields of enquiry interested in the same phenomena, a readiness to see the results of its enquiries used in the exploration of those complex problems which defy the resources of any one discipline. Conceived of as an agency for the mediation of knowledge, a discipline would reveal a willingness to forego the luxury

51

of treating enquiries as necessarily self-sufficient. It would reveal a willingness to tolerate indeterminate boundaries between what is 'pure' and what 'applied', and to make use of a range of different approaches chosen according to the nature of the particular problem at hand. Above all, it would show a willingness to tolerate the messiness of real events, because the story that needs to be told is a 'story about real life', and real life has a habit of slipping out of the door when human science focuses too closely upon the elegance, simplicity and rigour of research design.

I have said that I see Language Study as a process. In this sense, it goes one stage beyond the broad view of a discipline as an agency, because it exists in order to mediate between the disciplines which have something to say about language and the people who need to understand the true story about language as it is used for teaching and learning. In this sense, and unlike a discipline, Language Study does not ask questions unique to itself, nor does it have techniques of enquiry peculiar to itself. Its 'content' is not a content which the syllabus maker could ever draw a line around and say that these things and these alone constitute 'the foundations of the subject'. What it does do is provide a meeting point between the questions concerning language and the use of language, which arise in the context of teaching and learning, and the disciplines which might well be able to offer some contribution towards their answers. 'Might be able' is not a polite circumlocution. It points to the fact that one of the most important tasks for Language Study is to show that some key questions do not have answers as yet. For example, we do not yet know how human beings go on extending their command of a language after its initial acquisition. Putting together what we do know about such a question, however, can be very useful. It enables us to suggest what a definitive answer might look like and this can carry us well beyond the limits of our habitual assumptions about the problem.

Language Study also has to show that some of the questions about language which teachers most often ask are so formed that they can never have answers. Two examples must suffice. Those who look to linguistics for a justification of their belief in an absolute form of the language, against which all usage can be properly measured, with the faulty found wanting, will be disappointed, because they will find that natural language does not work like that. Those who hope to find a justification for their views about fluent and slovenly speech, good and bad accent, rich and impoverished dialects, by taking a linguistic view of language,

52

will be equally disappointed, because they will find that their questions about speech, accent and dialect are complex questions involving social and cultural, as well as linguistic, patterns rather than simple questions about the elements and structure of a particular language.

My last point is to link what has been said in this chapter about the design for Language Study to the climate created by a changing society. As society is subject to a process of continuous and rapid change, and the educational system reflects this process, the questions that teachers and learners ask will necessarily change also. Even if the questions themselves were to remain the same it is very unlikely that the relevant answers would remain the same. This situation implies the need for a very great flexibility in the process of relating the questions from the educational context to the disciplines which might be able to provide the answers. It suggests a willingness to discard what has been learnt, to review the relevance of what has *seemed* useful, and to realign in new configurations and relationships the components of old and tried answers. It also requires a willingness to assert the urgency of the new question over the institutional convenience of the received answer. In a changing world, it is better to know that you are asking the relevant question than comfort yourself that you have an impeccable answer to a problem that no longer exists.

5. 'God's truth' and 'hocus-pocus'

I want to end this chapter by looking at some of the problems which confront us when we set out to develop a design for Language Study, problems which arise from the nature of curriculum development rather than from the contingencies of class-room practice. The first of these is the great diversity we find in teacher education. In this country alone, it is so great that there sometimes seems to be as many different approaches to the education of teachers as there are institutions and agencies to provide that education. When we consider the practice of other countries in addition, the diversity becomes quite daunting. In these circumstances, it is necessary to focus upon the *design* for a particular approach rather than the details of particular courses and syllabuses. What is needed is a clear statement of the components which make up the approach and the principles which have led to their selection. With both of these available to them, those who wished to develop a Language Study approach would be in a position to

53

work out for themselves how best the components could be realized in terms of the actual courses and syllabuses that would meet the particular needs of their own learning situations.

To speak of a principled basis for selecting the components which will go to make up the framework of a particular approach raises the question of what we mean by the phrase 'developing an approach to'. One very common response to 'developing an approach to' is to see it as a matter of fitting together various items from different sources in order to produce a programme for class-room use. The emphasis is upon the list of different bits and pieces in the kit rather than the models that can be made with them, and there is no scope for asking whether these bits and pieces are the most suitable for building those models or why we should want to build these models rather than any others. This is to say that a course put together in this way lacks 'necessity'. There is no way of relating any part of it to an underlying theory or set of postulates which could provide a rational classification for putting the course together in one way rather than another.

To many people, a lack of necessity for what they put into their courses and syllabuses does not seem to matter. Perhaps they would even regard it as irrelevant so long as their choice of content or approach 'worked in the class-room'. Leaving aside for the moment the very difficult question as to how we know that something 'works', I would want to argue that the climate of change in the educational system has created a new situation in which it is much more important than ever to know what we are actually doing in a learning situation, and why we are doing it. This is because we need to see how a particular pattern of work matches up to the actual needs of learners, and those needs are no longer a fixed quantity, because they reflect the pattern of continuous cultural change.

In this situation, we need to be able to ask three basic questions about any pattern of work set up within the educational system: why were these features selected rather than any others? what was the total range of alternatives from which these features were selected? what objectives are to be served by the features selected? To answer these questions successfully involves course and syllabus having a principled basis, an explicit formulation of the theory which underlies their content and their organization. This would enable us to formulate answers to our three basic questions that did have 'necessity' and avoid some of the commonest answers which we offer at present: that the course has always had these things in

54

it; that the students like it; that that is how students/examiners/ Board of Studies/University/society/God/wants it to be; that that is all we can teach; that that is the only way we know how to teach; that anything else would be contrary to the Laws of Nature. All or any of which may be good and sufficient reasons for doing what we are doing, but they do not really help to justify the existing elements and structure of course or syllabus, unless they are derived from *an explicit set of principles* which relate content and organization to an underlying explanatory theory.

The question of why teachers and learners do what they do is not a theoretical question that concerns only the professional curriculum developer, but a severely practical matter that involves everyone who has to create patterns of activity for learning situations. Let me demonstrate this point by referring to the aim of this book. It sets out to show that a Language Study approach is relevant to the needs of teachers and learners. In effect, its argument invites the reader to assess for himself how far he needs a Language Study approach to make sense of his work as a teacher, and how far he considers such an approach relevant to the language needs of all learners. The book puts the reader in a position to do this by making explicit the theoretical basis for what it advocates. The reader will reach his decision on the relevance of what is offered, therefore, according to his assessment of the validity of the theory that guides the selection of the components and the objectives which are presented to him as the constituents of a Language Study approach. In this sense, what looks like an abstract question for the professional curriculum developer ends up by being a highly relevant practical question for the individual teacher, because it is the presence of an explicit principled basis for Language Study which allows him to judge for himself, on rational grounds, whether or not he wants to have anything to do with it.

The first three chapters of this book explored certain major aspects of man as a languaging animal, and as a social and cultural animal, in order to show that a connection can be made between the way men use language to live and the language needs of all teachers and learners. The implication was that there are certain conclusions about the part played by language in teaching and learning which can be seen to follow *necessarily* from the nature and function of language in the life and society of man. These conclusions constitute a theory of language which provides us with the principled basis for the Language Study approach that this book advocates. What follows in Chapter 5, therefore, is an explicit working out of this basis so that the reader can test the validity of that basis for himself. Only then does it make sense for him to go on and consider what this approach could offer him in terms of his own situation.

In setting out this basis, I make use of twelve postulates which can guide us in our selection of a number of relevant areas of enquiry for Language Study. This is a useful way of formulating a principled basis, because it enables the reader to see the whole foundation of the argument set out in a relatively short space so that the relationship between its different elements stands out clearly. There is a danger in doing it this way, however, because it is always easy to overlook the fact that a set of postulates of this kind is only one out of the number of possible sets which could have been offered. If I stress the fact that what I offer is only one out of a number of possibilities, however, I lay myself open to the charge that what I offer is of no value, because it is not *the* answer to the problem.

There is an old debate in Linguistics as to whether the linguist is trying to reveal God's truth about a language through his description of it, or merely using his own hocus-pocus of a linguistic theory to set out one possible version of the facts as far as that language is concerned. I think it will be obvious to all readers that I would be the last person to claim God's truth for anything I was putting forward. What I am offering is one possible version of the facts as far as the development of an approach to Language Study is concerned. I hold very strongly to the view that all theories are *arbitrary* in the sense that all we can ever hope to do in our explorations of some aspect of reality, linguistic or social or cultural, is to offer one version out of the several alternative versions the facts make possible. We put this version together according to our own reading of the facts, and in doing so, we necessarily adopt only one out of a number of possible alternative ways of viewing the aspect of reality with which we are concerned. We put forward this version, and invite others to question its validity. The only constraint we have to accept in taking up this invitation is that that there is no point in trying to assess the validity of one version by using the theoretical postulates of another. We won't get very far if we insist on judging one man's hocus-pocus according to the dictates of our own belief in God's truth.

Let me end by trying to relate this argument to the quotation from Professor Medawar on page 50. He says that we start an enquiry by postulating '. . . a logically articulated structure of justifiable beliefs about nature'. In our case, this 'articulated structure' is the principled basis for a Language Study approach. Medawar insists, however, that this structure is only a story about a *Possible* World. In other words we are implying that if these and these facts are indeed true, then this is what one aspect of the world, or reality, really looks like. As he says, 'it is a story, which we *invent*', but he also says that it is a story which we 'criticise and modify *as we go along*', so that 'it ends by being . . . a story about *real life*' (My italics). This is the argument for putting forward at this stage in time an account of Language Study in terms of its principled basis and the components which can be derived from that basis, because we must begin by inventing our Possible World of Language Study, and then proceed to criticize and modify it as we try to make it approximate more and more closely to what would be, in terms of the language needs of teachers and learners, 'a story about real life'. This we can only do if we can see what principles shape the plot, the characters and the action of the story, because it is to these *principles* that the modifying criticism of others must be directed, if they have alternative stories to tell, and not to the detail of the courses that could be derived from them.

5 A Design for Language Study

1. The principled basis

The last chapter set out the framework of the design for Language Study which this book advocates. In order to provide the necessary support and guidance for the development of particular courses and syllabuses, there are four aspects of this framework which have to be set out in detail:

1) A *theory of language* which will provide the principled basis for the particular approach to Language Study which I am advocating.
2) A set of *components* which will provide an *operational focus* for Language Study.
3) A set of *areas of concern* which will define an *operational domain* for Language Study.
4) A set of *objectives* by which the activities in learning situations that Language Study gives rise to may be guided, and their effectiveness assessed.

The distinction I am proposing here between an *operational focus* and an *operational domain* is a distinction between the way in which we show interest in a particular aspect of reality and the human activities which give rise to that interest. The *components* of Language Study, which make up its *operational focus*, provide the framework within which we can formulate the kinds of questions about the nature and function of language that we want to ask, because we are interested in the use of language in the context of teaching and learning. On the other hand, the *areas of concern*, which arise out of this interest, reveal the source of those questions in terms of actual personal, cultural, social and educational contexts and thus provide us with an *operational domain* for Language Study. It is the possibility of setting up such a domain which provides the justification for the claim of Language Study to be considering questions that are not explored elsewhere.

Our point of departure, then, must be the statement of a theory of language which is derived from disciplines which have something to say about man the speaking animal. In *Exploring Language*, I have suggested that a theory of *language* is not the same thing as a theory of *linguistic description*. It is a:

> . . . rational and explicit attempt to answer questions which ask *why language is as it is*, rather than *what one particular language contains or how its parts fit together*.

A theory of language must try to explain the patterns of natural languages in terms of the use that their speakers make of them. I have implied throughout this book that this is the only theory of language which can provide the basis for an exploration of the needs of teachers and learners as users of language, because it focuses attention upon language as the medium through which men make themselves and their society.

An outline for a theory of this kind appears in *Exploring Language*, Chapter Seven. A linguistic basis for it can be found in the volume of papers by Professor M. A. K. Halliday, in this series; a biological basis for it is offered in the forthcoming volume in the series by Roger Gurney; and the social and cultural basis will be explored further in another volume in the series by my wife and myself. All I need do in this context, therefore, is to present the fundamental postulates about the nature and function of language upon which the theory rests. While there are many different ways of formulating these postulates, and while each is open to a range of widely differing interpretations in terms of an operational theory of linguistic description, the substance of what they say about man as a languaging animal would be needed by any theory capable of justifying a Language Study approach.

Beginning with language itself, we can say:

1) That a language is a very complex autonomous organization, involving a finite number of elements, which can be combined in different ways, according to a statable set of rules, in order to yield a finite number of types of structure.

2) That, however, this self-consistent and finite organization is a symbolic system capable of producing an unlimited

number of utterances differing in meaning from each other.

3) That there is a set of rules, moreover, which governs the relationship between structures and meanings of such a kind that utterances are *predictable*, in the sense that speakers of the same language are able to derive meaning from them, and at the same time *original*, in the sense that the meanings expressed by these utterances may be unique to them.

4) That using this symbolic system to make utterances involves ' ... a simultaneous selection from among a large number of interrelated options (which) represent the "meaning potential" of language'.

M. A. K. Halliday

The activity of languaging, therefore, consists in the use of a self-consistent symbol system to convert 'meaning potential' into meaningful utterance and to derive meaningfulness from the 'meaning potential' encoded in the utterances of others. The essential thing to grasp about language is that it is composed of a large store of many different types of 'elements and structure', invariable in their nature and function, which can be put together, by the act of languaging, to meet the needs of innumerable unique situations. This act of languaging is guided by rules which determine what choices of 'elements and structure' are available to the speaker in making any particular utterance: 'inventiveness' enters into the situation in so far as the speaker *has to* exercise a process of choice in order to fashion any utterance. The 'elements and structure' may be given, but their deployment in actual utterances is open to limitless individual variations along many dimensions of difference.

If we now focus on the idea of man as a languaging animal, we can add the following postulates about language as a form of behaviour unique to human beings. We can say:

5) That language has survival value for the species; consequently there is a biological basis for the capacity to language which will be found in the genetic design of human beings.

6) That a *particular* language is learnt, however, by individual human beings in the course of continuous interaction with other human beings, who already possess an operational command of that language.

That is, an individual speaker's capacity to language is the product of a genetically-programmed potential for learning a natural language exercised in a particular and local human environment, personal, social and cultural.

If we now consider the individual user of a language, we can suggest,

7) That an individual uses language to discriminate between one experience and the next; he calls upon the categories of his language for classifying and recording what he experiences; and he makes use of the resources of the symbolic system in his possession to understand what it is that he has experienced.

8) That an individual's capacity *to know himself as an individual*, his ability to develop a sense of *self*, a personal identity that is uniquely his, because it differentiates him from all other individuals, is a function of his capacity to language.

These two postulates reinforce the central importance of the fact that learning a language and learning how to use a language are intimately bound up with who we are, and where, and when, and in what manner, we grow up, because we *are* our language.

Man is a cultural animal, however, and language is the primary means available to him for the transmission of the values, capabilities and habits which go to make up a culture. It has been said already that acquiring a capacity to language is the same thing as acquiring a capacity to make meanings. Therefore we can say:

9) That, as the meanings we acquire are necessarily those that have currency amongst the individuals with whom we interact in the process of learning our language, learning a language is necessarily a form of cultural learning.

10) That the acquisition and use of language is a function of communities; that the use of language required by the exercise of capabilities and habits is the active life of communities; and that the part played by language in mediating the values is the continuity of communities.

This is to say that communities provide the immediate environment for man as a cultural animal; and that language is the essential cohesive element in the formation and perpetuation of individual communities.

Man is also a social animal, and consequently we must consider how '. . . language functions as a link in concerted human activity . . .' (Malinowski): that is, how language enables men

61

to sustain patterns of behaviour that are social and interactional. We can say:

11) That men use language in order to initiate and maintain relationships with each other; to exercise control over each others' actions and thoughts; to create social groups which are able to maintain their coherence and identity over extended periods of time; and to articulate the larger structures required by collective social action.

12) That, as relationships are patterns of social action which occur in particular social settings, and as we learn how to language by our activity in particular social settings, the settings we have known will play a large part in shaping the way in which we use language to relate to others, and to exercise control over them.

This is to suggest that language functions for us successfully in so far as it is public rather than private. Its value to us in terms of survival derives from its capability as a symbolic system which can convert 'meaning potential' into *meanings potentially accessible to any other speaker of the language*, solely by virtue of their being speakers of the language. There is a final paradox in this, however. While language is a symbolic system for making public meanings upon which the whole fabric of human life depends, it is also each individual human being's most intimate and private possession, the system he uses to symbolize a unique view of the world. In our approach to Language Study we must never lose sight of either view.

2. The components of Language Study

These twelve postulates provide us, then, with the principled basis which supports this particular framework for an approach to Language Study. We cannot move easily from a set of theoretical statements at this level of abstraction, however, to the detailed provision of courses and syllabuses. In order to do so, we need to set up a middle ground which will relate our principles to what we decide to put into our actual programmes of work, so that they will not lack necessity. This middle ground comprises a set of *components* for Language Study, which derive from our principled basis, and a number of *areas of concern*, from which we derive the questions about language in teaching and learning that we wish to explore.

Let us look now at these components. As I have suggested, they are not 'subjects', or even subject contents, but a set of specific points of focus upon the nature and function of language. They can be formulated in the following terms:

I. Language as a function of its own internal organization as a self-consistent symbolic system, and the way in which that system is related to 'meaning potential' on the one hand, and modes of expression on the other.

II. Language as a generalized capacity, genetically-programmed and specific to man as a species. (A focus upon the degree to which language exists, because there is survival value in being a talking animal.)

III. Language in the creation and projection of the self. (A focus upon the degree to which we are dependent upon language for our capacity to make sense of the world and transmit our understanding of it to others.)

IV. Language as the medium for invention, mediation and modification of the values, capabilities and habits that make up a culture.

V. Language as the means of initiating, maintaining and controlling relationships with others. (A focus upon the basis of our ability to create social groups and articulate social structures.)

In developing a framework for our approach to Language Study, we can then ask a sequence of three basic questions in respect of each of these five components:

1) What is there to say about this aspect of the nature and function of language in so far as we are focused upon the general question of man's use of language to live?

2) How can we relate what we learn about this aspect of language to the particular questions we want to ask about the language needs of all learners?

3) What are the implications of this enquiry for the organization of activities in learning situations and the structure of their environment in schools and colleges?

Alternatively, we could phrase these questions so that we ask of each component:

1) What is the case, if we want to know how men use language *for living?*

2) What follows, therefore, if we want to know how men use *language for learning?*
3) What follows from this, if our aim is to develop a linguistic perspective on language for teachers and learners relevant to the needs of formal learning situations?

What I want to do next is to take each of the five components in turn and suggest how we might formulate more specific questions under the general heading of the first of our three basic questions, 'What is the case, if we want to know how men use *language for living?*

I—*Language as a self-consistent symbolic system*
1) What can formal linguistic descriptions tell us about the way in which 'meaning potential' is realized in terms of particular configurations of 'elements and structure'?
2) What would such a description have to say about the range of options open to the speaker at a particular point of utterance?
3) How do the elements and structure of this system relate to the sounds we make in the air and the marks we make on the page; and what is the relationship between these two modes of expression?

II—*Language as a phenomenon specific to the species*
1) What is the relationship between brain process and language production?
2) What is the relationship between the maturation of the organism and the development of a capacity to language?
3) What are the biological bases for the malfunction or breakdown in this capacity to language?

III—*Language as the medium for individuation*
1) How does the individual make use of language to categorize, order and interpret his experience of the world?
2) How does he use language to develop, maintain, project and modify a sense of self; and what part does language play in enabling us to perceive of ourselves as being *the same person,* irrespective of a multiplicity of local changes in time, space and situation?
3) How does he use language to create Possible Worlds; and how does he use language to express a unique view of the world?

IV—*Language and culture*
  1) What part does language play in the process of transmitting culture from one generation to the next?
  2) What do we mean by cultural learning and how closely is it initially bound up with our learning of a language?
  3) What problems arise out of the way in which we use language to mediate values when a society no longer possesses a unitary culture?

V—*Language and social action*
  1) What is the role of language in interaction; how do we use it to relate ourselves to others and what constraints does this place upon our freedom of action as individual selves?
  2) What is the relationship between verbal and non-verbal channels in the context of face-to-face interaction?
  3) To what extent are patterns of social action patterns of language in use; and how do we create these patterns of language in use in order to serve our needs as members of social groups and organizations?

What I have tried to do in presenting these questions is to indicate the kind of enquiry into the nature and function of language which is relevant to the particular context of Language Study. Exploring the answers to any one of them should be carried out bearing in mind the basic aim for Language Study, the development of a linguistic perspective. The aim is not to find out the facts for their own sake, but to discover what is relevant to a better understanding of the language needs of learning and teaching.

Each one of the questions I have enumerated would constitute a major theme in itself. The next stage is to break down each question into a large number of much more specific questions that would point to local and concrete enquiries into particular topics. A reader who would like to see how this can be done should take a look at *Language in Use*, the approach to Language Study which I and my colleagues developed for the Schools Council in this country. It is a resource for the teacher, which suggests how he can initiate Language Study for the pupil or student by working from their own existing intuitions about, and understanding of, language. For those who might already know the volume, and for those who might be interested enough to consult it, I would point out that four of the five components I have discussed in this

65

section relate directly to the structure of *Language in Use* in the following way:

Language in Use	*Language Study Component*
Part I. Language, its nature and function.	I. Language as a self-consistent symbolic system.
Part II. Language and the Individual.	III. Language as the medium for individuation.
Part III. Language and Social Man.	IV. Language as the medium for cultural action.
	V. Language as the medium for social action.

3. Areas of concern

So far in this chapter, I have been looking at the framework for a Language Study approach from the direction of the theory of language that provides it with a principled basis from which we can derive its components. I want now to look at this framework from the opposite direction, the *areas of concern* which give us the questions we want to ask about language in teaching and learning.

Let me now suggest six of these areas of concern. I think I have made it clear already that a list of this kind is not an exhaustive account of what might concern Language Study, but a *minimum* set of possibilities, those areas of concern which no approach to Language Study could properly afford to overlook. They are:

1) The nature and function of language as a medium for teaching and learning.
2) The activities of teachers and learners as users of language for learning.
3) The character of the contexts in which language is used for teaching and learning.
4) The question of extending the learner's command over language for living and language for learning.
5) The question of developing pupils' awareness of how they use language to live and language to learn.
6) The question of developing a reflexive linguistic perspective for teachers.

Each of these primary areas of concern can be made to yield a number of much more specific topics which would form the basis for particular explorations. Let me show what this might look

66

like by taking (2), the language activity of teachers and pupils as participants in learning situations.

If we take the teacher first, we need to consider the way in which he creates a climate for learning through his decisions about what is to be learnt, and how it is to be learnt. We have to focus upon the linguistic implications of the fact that:

1) He determines the local content of what his pupils and students are expected to learn.
2) His own use of language, and the materials he provides, determine the character of the language through which his pupils or students gain access to that content.
3) It is his own attitudes towards the language for learning he expects his pupils or students to use, whether he reveals them implicitly or explicitly, that determine the character of the language for learning they will believe it possible to use.
4) The attitudes and assumptions he reveals, implicitly or explicitly, about language for living, set the limits within which his pupils or students feel free to draw upon their knowledge of the language as competent native speakers in order to participate in the learning situation.

If we now look at the learner, we can suggest that, as a participant in a learning situation, he is expected to:

1) Master a content, which he does not normally provide himself.
2) Make sense of this content through the use of a language for learning, which he does not himself select.
3) Render an account of the success of his learning, spoken or written, using this same language for learning.

At the same time, we can say that he will certainly bring into the learning situation:

4) His own folk-linguistic intuitions about the kind of language he expects to have to use for learning, and about the kind of language which he believes to be acceptable in the context of a learning situation.
5) His own attitudes and assumptions about the way in which people use language to live.

It seems to me that we could formulate two basic objectives which a Language Study approach might derive from this

67

breakdown of one aspect of a key *area of concern*. As far as the teacher is concerned, the objective is to put him in a position to answer for himself, in relation to his own learning situation, the following question:

> How can I create a situation in my own class-room that will give my pupils the incentive and the opportunity to develop the operational command of the language for learning that they need; and how can I best draw upon their existing command of language for living in the process?

As far as the learner is concerned, there is a dual objective:

1) To create a situation in which he can develop an appropriate command of the language for learning which he needs and an accompanying awareness of how he uses language to learn.
2) To use the learning situation to develop his overall command of language for living by developing his awareness of how he uses language to live.

4. Objectives

At the end of the preceding section, we were in a position to see how the examination of one particular area of concern and its breakdown into a number of specific topics or questions led us to formulate two particular objectives for a Language Study approach. I do not have the space to provide a detailed breakdown for the other areas of concern, but I can suggest two particular objectives for each of them. Taken together, the twelve objectives will then provide us with an overall picture of the specific contributions Language Study would hope to make to a better understanding of the part played by language in teaching and learning.

In order to fulfil the claims that we make for it, let us say then that Language Study would have to show how we could reach the following local and particular objectives.

In relation to the first of our areas of concern, the nature and function of language as a medium for teaching and learning, we can suggest these two objectives:

1) To show what characterizes the varieties of language, ways

of speaking as well as ways of writing, that arise specifically in the context of school or college.

2) To show how these varieties of a language relate to the ways in which it is used for living in the context of family, community and society.

The second of our areas, the activities of teachers and learners as users of language for learning, has already been dealt with at the end of the preceding section. Our third area, however, yields us these two possible objectives:

3) To show what personal, cultural, social and linguistic factors brought into the learning situation by teacher and learner do most to determine the climate for language activity.

4) To show what the school or college as a social organization contributes to this climate.

The question of extending command over language for living and language for learning is the fourth of our areas of concern. From this, we can derive these two objectives:

5) To make available a theory of competence which would provide a principled basis for developing activities and procedures designed to encourage growth of competence.

6) To enable the teacher to use such a theory in order to assess the effectiveness of the language activity in his own situation, judged from the point of view of its contribution to the growth of competence.

The fifth is closely related to the fourth, the question of developing pupils' awareness of how they use language to live and to learn. This would give us the following objectives:

7) To demonstrate the degree to which the success of language activity in learning situations depends upon the attitudes of teachers and learners towards language for learning.

8) To show how the development of awareness in the use of language for learning is related to a prior development of awareness in the use of language for living, and how growth of competence is also related to this dual development.

Our sixth and last area of concern specifically involves teachers. In a sense, the question of a reflexive linguistic perspective for teachers is the logical outcome of the other five. Given that we accept the validity of the objectives so far enumerated, then it is hard to avoid the conclusion that they require of the teacher a particularly developed awareness of the nature and function of language. Let us, therefore, suggest these two objectives for our final area of concern:

9) To show what knowledge about the nature and function of language is most relevant to the context of language in teaching and learning, and where that knowledge may be obtained.

10) To show how teachers might be able to develop a linguistic perspective and what difference it would make to their class-room practice were they to do so.

I would stress the fact that these ten objectives represent only one way of formulating the questions involved. At the same time, I do not think an approach to Language Study which ignored the substance of these ten would provide a very satisfactory mediator between the language problems of teachers and learners and the sources which might be able to produce answers for them. I would also say that we could take each of these objectives and break it down further, either in terms of what Language Study ought to provide or what teachers and learners could be expected to achieve by working towards that objective.

While I do not have the space to deal with each one of these objectives in such detail, I would like to take one of them, (7), and suggest what the pursuit of this objective might make available to the teacher:

1) It would put him in a position to see that pupils and students can only meet the demands made by language for learning if they are free to bring into the learning situation, and make use of it, their native speakers' command of language for living.

2) It would demonstrate to him that this is only possible where there is congruence between their understanding of how they use language to live and their understanding of what it means to use language to learn.

3) It would make him aware of his own fundamental contribution to the language of the learning situation in terms of:
    i) His folk-linguistic attitudes towards language and the use of language.

ii) His customary professional view of the use of language for living.

iii) His awareness of the linguistic attitudes and assumptions which his pupils or students bring into the learning situation and their probable divergence from his own.

4) It would make him aware of his own use of language in terms of:

    i) What he says, formally through instruction, informally through consultation and advice, and in his exercise of social control.

    ii) What written text he makes available or recommends.

    iii) What demands he makes upon his pupils' and students' capacity to language, spoken or written.

I want to end this section by formulating a *global aim* for this approach to Language Study, an aim which would define its particular contribution to the professional competence of all teachers. The objectives I have described in this section can only be realized in so far as teachers are able to modify their customary ways of regarding language, whether for living or for learning. Collectively, therefore, they suggest that Language Study must be concerned with the development of a linguistic perspective. This gives a global aim and we can set it out in the following terms:

1) A teacher needs to understand the part played by language in the work of every area of the curriculum, whatever his own particular responsibilities.

2) He must be able to assess his individual contribution to the language climate of school or college in terms of:

    i) His own individual language activity, inside and outside the learning situation.

    ii) The activity he demands and expects from all the pupils and students with whom he comes into contact.

3) He needs to understand the part language plays in every aspect of our lives as human beings, personal, cultural and social.

4) He must be aware of the intimate relationship between the two aspects of language in use, language for living and language for learning.

What follows in section five is an outline of the evidence the work of the Schools Council *Language in Use* Project provides for suggesting how we can begin to work towards such an aim.

5. The evidence from the *Language in Use* project

This project set out to develop a Language Study approach to work in English at pupil level. Some of its effects upon teachers who used it are, however, relevant to the present context. Through their actual work in the class-room, based upon pupil's own existing experience of using language and employing a thorough-going exploratory approach, they came to review their whole attitude to language in the class-room context and beyond.

In their comments and reports, six points consistently recurred:

1) Language Study was accepted as relevant to their pupils' problems, and their own, in connection with the use of language for learning and teaching.

2) Their own folk linguistic attitudes had come to be considerably modified. Three factors seemed particularly important in making this possible:

   i) Continuous use of *Language in Use* teaches about language as it teaches: in other words, teachers learn as much as pupils by the same process of involvement in the exploration of their own experience as users of language.

   ii) Starting with pupils' own experience of using language to live powerfully modifies the idea that they do not know how to use language properly until they are taught to do so at school.

   iii) Looking at language as a human activity reveals the degree to which many common class-room problems are basically *linguistic* problmes.

3) Using the units of *Language in Use* involves teachers in using the theory of language implicit in their design. As they grow more familiar with the theory, they come to see its relevance to their work and want to know more, initially, about the principles underlying the units, but ultimately about the nature and function of language itself.

4) Teachers find that this familiarity with the theory also comes to provide them with a conceptual framework that they can use to shape the questions about language which they want to ask and into which they can fit the answers they discover.

5) In effect, they find that this framework gives them the rudiments of a principled approach to the linguistic aspects of their work and thus provides:
   i) A means of assessing the potential of any activity in terms of its ability to generate in pupils the command of language for learning necessary for its effective pursuit.
   ii) A means of planning an approach to his own and his pupils' use of language that is consonant with what we know to be true about its nature and function.
   iii) A basis for assessing the relative contributions of all subjects to the pupils' linguistic competence and the particular nature of the contribution properly to be expected from the English Department.

6) Using the units provides a first-hand experience of using an approach that is ordered and coherent, yet does not impose rigid structure and direction upon the pattern of work that derives from it.

Given that this is what happened when the units were used in the ordinary course of day-to-day teaching, we can necessarily ask why it happened. These results were possible because of certain features in the basic design. For our present purposes they can be summarized as:

1) A formal framework for 'content' that offered:
   i) Flexibility within a rational ordering of options so that a multiplicity of individual 'courses' can be built up from the units.
   ii) A principled basis for selecting options.
   iii) A rationale for any work undertaken.

2) A notion of 'content' that broke away from the idea that the study of language in the class-room must *necessarily* show the same kind of explicitness of analytical statement common in other subject areas.

3) A pattern of class-room activity that enables both teacher and pupils to learn new ways of operating together in the process of following out a clearly defined objective. The focus is upon the enquiry and the 'new ways' seem to arise naturally out of the work to be done.

4) Objectives for the units that combine growth of awareness of the nature and function of language with growth of competence in the use of spoken and written English.

5) An overall strategy where the aim was to create patterns of work that would modify attitudes. You cannot *tell* people what to think about language, because it is too intimate and familiar a possession; therefore you have to let them work towards a situation in which they come to see for themselves the limits of their existing views. The key process, here, is the 'working towards', the process of the enquiry itself.

Part II
A Guide to Reading in Language Study

by
Geoffrey Thornton

Introduction

The suggestions made in this second part of the book do not claim to constitute either an exhaustive or a definitive list of books concerned with various aspects of Language Study. They represent a selection of those books available at the time of writing (April 1972) which the authors have found particularly helpful, not only in their own reading in the subject but also in the course of their work with teachers. The books and articles referred to are grouped in sections to correspond with the schema described in chapter 5, section II. In each case a book will be identified by the author's name and title (e.g. HALLIDAY: EXPLORATIONS IN THE FUNCTIONS OF LANGUAGE), with full bibliographical details given in an appendix.

1. Language as a self-consistent symbolic system

Two essays in SAPIR: CULTURE, LANGUAGE AND PERSONALITY make a good starting point—the first, called simply 'Language', and the third, 'The Status of Linguistics as a Science'. The first chapter, 'Introductory: Language Defined' of SAPIR: LANGUAGE, which is subtitled 'An Introduction to the Study of Speech' also makes good introductory reading.

Commonly held, if frequently fallacious, views of language are sometimes called 'folk-linguistic notions of language'. (See DOUGHTY, PEARCE, THORNTON: EXPLORING LANGUAGE, chapters 1 and 2.) The contrast between the folk-linguistic view and the view of language held by the linguist is pointed out in chapters 2 and 3 of CRYSTAL: LINGUISTICS. Chapter 3 is followed by 'Interlude: An Example', a most readable attempt to illustrate concretely some of the 'hallmarks of a scientifically responsible approach to language study'. In the first two chapters of PALMER: GRAMMAR will also be found some comparison between 'traditional' notions about language and those now held by the linguists. For further reading see the introduction to (Ed.) LYONS: NEW HORIZONS IN LINGUISTICS, where the editor discusses some of the 'key concepts of modern linguistics'.

For a brief introduction to phonetics and phonology see CRYSTAL: LINGUISTICS, pp. 167–86. This may be followed by the introductory chapter, and chapters 2 and 3, of CHAO: LANGUAGE AND SYMBOLIC SYSTEMS, and chapter 3 of LYONS: INTRODUCTION TO THEORETICAL LINGUISTICS. ABERCROMBIE: ELEMENTS OF GENERAL PHONETICS gives a good, comprehensive account. For a description of the way in which intonation functions as part of the grammar of spoken English, see HALLIDAY: INTONATION AND GRAMMAR IN BRITISH ENGLISH.

A short introductory course of reading in syntax might begin with CRYSTAL: LINGUISTICS, pp. 187–230; CHAO, chapter 4; LYONS: INTRODUCTION TO THEORETICAL LINGUISTICS, chapters 4 and 5; and PALMER: GRAMMAR, already referred to.

For a short introduction to the concept of 'meaning potential' (p. 60) see 'The problem of meaning', a chapter in FIRTH: THE TONGUES OF MEN & SPEECH, and THORNTON, BIRK AND HUDSON: LANGUAGE AT WORK. The papers which comprise HALLIDAY: EXPLORATIONS IN THE FUNCTIONS OF LANGUAGE (in this series) bring together a number of related treatments of the idea. See also HALLIDAY: 'LANGUAGE STRUCTURE AND LANGUAGE FUNCTION' in (Ed.) LYONS: NEW HORIZONS IN LINGUISTICS, and HALLIDAY: 'LEARNING HOW TO MEAN'.

For a discussion of the relationship between "the sounds we make in the air and the marks we make on the page" see CHAO, chapter 8. For a description of the writing system of English see ALBROW: THE ENGLISH WRITING SYSTEM. Related to this, but with specific reference to the teaching of reading and writing is the Teachers' Manual to MACKAY, THOMPSON AND SCHAUB: BREAK-THROUGH TO LITERACY.

2. Language as a phenomenon specific to the species

Introductory reading—GURNEY: LANGUAGE, BRAIN AND INTER-ACTIVE PROCESSES (in this series).

The work of E. H. Lenneberg is perhaps the best known in this area. See LENNEBERG: 'A BIOLOGICAL PERSPECTIVE OF

LANGUAGE' in (Ed.) OLDFIELD and MARSHALL: LANGUAGE, and his book LENNEBERG: THE BIOLOGICAL FOUNDATIONS OF LANGUAGE.

For reading in the biological background, see NATHAN: THE NERVOUS SYSTEM, and WOOLDRIDGE: THE MACHINERY OF THE BRAIN. Also GREGORY: THE INTELLIGENT EYE (especially chapter 8).

For a series of readings on the impact of biological factors on the individual's potential for language acquisition see Part Two (Biological Factors) of (Ed.) HUDSON: THE ECOLOGY OF HUMAN INTELLIGENCE, and the section called 'From Biology' in (Ed.) RICHARDSON AND SPEARS: RACE, CULTURE AND INTELLIGENCE.

A survey of what is currently known about the mechanism of speech production and reception might begin with EXPLORING LANGUAGE, chapter 8, part i, followed by FRY: 'SPEECH RECEPTION AND PERCEPTION' and LAVER: 'THE PRODUCTION OF SPEECH', both in (Ed.) LYONS: NEW HORIZONS IN LINGUISTICS. GOLDMAN EISLER: PSYCHOLINGUISTICS gives an account of her research into the significance of hesitation pausing in fluent speech. On this, see also BOOMER: 'HESITATION PAUSING AND GRAMMATICAL ENCODING' in (Ed.) OLDFIELD AND MARSHALL: LANGUAGE.

For an introduction to the literature of language disorders, see LENNEBERG: 'SPEECH AS A MOTOR SKILL WITH SPECIAL REFERENCE TO NON-APHASIC DISORDERS' in (Ed.) PRIBRAM: ADAPTATION and TALLAND: DISORDERS OF MEMORY AND LEARNING.

WILKINSON: THE FOUNDATIONS OF LANGUAGE brings together a great deal of information on many related topics. See particularly, in this area, chapters 6 and 7.

3. Language as a medium for individuation

Introduction—EXPLORING LANGUAGE, chapters 3 and 4, and THORNTON: THE INDIVIDUAL'S DEVELOPMENT OF A LANGUAGE, in THORNTON, BIRK AND HUDSON: LANGUAGE AT WORK.

For discussion of the way in which the individual sets up categories in order to make sense of experience see ABERCROMBIE: THE ANATOMY OF JUDGMENT, chapters 2 and 3; LEACH: 'ANIMAL CATEGORIES AND VERBAL ABUSE' in (Ed.) LENNEBERG: NEW DIRECTIONS IN THE STUDY OF LANGUAGE, and BROWN: 'HOW SHALL A THING BE CALLED?' in (Ed.) OLDFIELD AND MARSHALL: LANGUAGE.

On problems attendant upon creating and maintaining a sense of self see GOFFMAN: STIGMA and GOFFMAN: THE PRESENTATION OF SELF IN EVERYDAY LIFE. See also BANNISTER AND FRANSELLA: INQUIRING MAN and BRITTON: LANGUAGE AND LEARNING, chapter 1.

FIRTH: 'PERSONALITY AND LANGUAGE IN SOCIETY' in his PAPERS IN LINGUISTICS, 1934–51 would form a good introduction to WHORF: LANGUAGE, THOUGHT AND REALITY, a collection of essays that has had an important influence on the arguments of the last ten years.

In BERGER AND LUCKMANN: THE SOCIAL CONSTRUCTION OF REALITY the authors explore the social foundations of what the individual comes to accept as reality.

Various influences contributing to the individual's construction of reality are examined in some of the readings in (Ed.) WISE-MAN: INTELLIGENCE AND ABILITY (see especially HEBB: 'THE GROWTH AND DECLINE OF INTELLIGENCE' and J. MCV. HUNT: 'INTELLIGENCE AND EXPERIENCE') and in (Ed.) HUDSON: THE ECOLOGY OF HUMAN INTELLIGENCE. See especially extracts number 12–16. HUDSON: FRAMES OF MIND follows HUDSON: CONTRARY IMAGINATIONS in looking at some of the factors predisposing the individual to one view of reality rather than another. Some recent points of controversy in this area are discussed in contributions to (Ed.) RICHARDSON AND SPEARS: RACE, CULTURE AND INTELLIGENCE.

4. Language as a medium for cultural action

SPROTT: HUMAN GROUPS provides a good introductory read to this section. It might be followed by SAPIR: LANGUAGE, chapter 10 and by a number of essays in SAPIR: CULTURE, LANGUAGE AND PERSONALITY.

HALL: THE SILENT LANGUAGE is a book which the author says 'is written for the layman . . . in such a way as to lead the reader gradually from the known to the unknown' and make him aware of the infinitely subtle ways in which culture is transmitted from generation to generation.

DOUGLAS: PURITY AND DANGER and DOUGLAS: NATURAL SYMBOLS discuss the symbolic significance in the life of society of such things as rules of hygiene.

The first part of (Ed.) HUDSON: THE ECOLOGY OF HUMAN IN-TELLIGENCE is called 'The Cultural Context'. See, especially, the first extract, D'ANDRADE: 'SEX DIFFERENCES AND CULTURAL INSTITUTIONS'.

In FRANKENBERG: COMMUNITIES IN BRITAIN the author brings together a number of studies of various kinds of community in Britain. See chapters 5 and 7. Chapter 9 contains very useful definitions of the sociologist's concepts of 'role' and 'network'. (See EXPLORING LANGUAGE, chapters 5 and 6). SHARP: ENGLISH IN A BI-LINGUAL COMMUNITY (in this series) explores the implications for those living in communities which have two languages of the relationship between those languages.

5. Language as the medium for social action

BERGER : INVITATION TO SOCIOLOGY makes a good introduction to the reading suggested in this section.

For discussion of recent work in socio-linguistics see PRIDE: THE SOCIAL MEANING OF LANGUAGE, chapters 1–7. The editorial introduction to GIGLIOLI: LANGUAGE AND SOCIAL CONTEXT reminds us that questions to be asked about the part played by language in social interaction may be summarized as, 'Who speaks to whom in what language and on what occasion?' The excerpts in Part Two of that volume, headed 'Speech and Situated Action', form a useful anthology.

The eighth excerpt is BERNSTEIN: 'SOCIAL CLASS, LANGUAGE AND SOCIALIZATION', which is also reprinted in BERNSTEIN: CLASS, CODES AND CONTROL, Vol. 1. This is a collection of Bernstein's writings over the last twelve years, prefaced by an introduction in which the author traces the development of his ideas during this period. BERNSTEIN: CLASS, CODES AND CONTROL, Vol. 2 will be a collection of papers by various authors on aspects of the relationship between social class and educability. See particularly HASAN: CODE, REGISTER AND SOCIAL DIALECT. See also LAWTON: SOCIAL CLASS, LANGUAGE AND EDUCATION for a discussion of the issues and a summary of relevant research up to the time of publication.

The relationship between society and its educational agencies (see p. 14) may be approached through some of the contributions in COSIN et al: SCHOOL AND SOCIETY, particularly sections I and II. The introduction to (Ed.) YOUNG: KNOWLEDGE AND CONTROL, followed by the first three pieces in the volume, will enable the exploration to be taken further. These are YOUNG's own 'AN APPROACH TO THE STUDY OF CURRICULA AS SOCIALLY ORGANISED KNOWLEDGE', BERNSTEIN: 'ON THE CLASSIFICATION AND FRAMING OF KNOWLEDGE' and ESLAND: 'TEACHING AND LEARNING AS THE ORGANISATION OF KNOWLEDGE.'

(Ed.) HOOPER: THE CURRICULUM is a collection concerned with the context, design and development of the curriculum, including such topics as 'Education and social change in modern England' and 'Freedom and learning: the need for choice'.

Section III of SCHOOL AND SOCIETY, entitled 'Learning and its organisation in school', contains half a dozen pieces which look at some of the ways in which the organization of schools affects those who go to them. This is also considered in HANNAM, SMYTH AND STEPHENSON: YOUNG TEACHERS AND RELUCTANT LEARNERS, and in some of the contributions to (Ed.) RUBINSTEIN AND STONEMAN: EDUCATION FOR DEMOCRACY. LETTER TO A TEACHER describes convincingly the way in which attitudes in school can discriminate against some categories of pupil.

There is a growing literature concerned with the school as an environment for language development. See, for example, BARNES AND BRITTON: LANGUAGE, THE LEARNER AND THE SCHOOL, BARNES: CLASSROOM CONTEXTS FOR LANGUAGE AND LEARNING and KEDDIE: 'CLASSROOM KNOWLEDGE' in (Ed.) YOUNG: KNOWLEDGE AND CONTROL. CREBER: LOST FOR WORDS provides a well-argued consideration of the connection between educational failure and the climate provided in the school for language use. See also POSTMAN AND WEINGARTNER: TEACHING AS A SUBVERSIVE ACTIVITY, especially chapter 7, 'Languaging', and, in this series, THORNTON: LANGUAGE, EXPERIENCE AND SCHOOL.

For a more specific consideration of language in discussion as a context for language development, see EXPLORING LANGUAGE, chapter 8, part ii; ABERCROMBIE: THE ANATOMY OF JUDGMENT, chapters 5 onwards; the relevant parts of BARNES AND BRITTON; and HANNAM, SMYTH AND STEPHENSON, chapter 6.

It might be useful at this stage to look at problems arising from folk-linguistic notions of dialect, accent and correctness. On accent and dialect see EXPLORING LANGUAGE, chapter 10; and—in ABERCROMBIE : STUDIES IN PHONETICS AND LINGUISTICS—the chapter entitled 'RP and Local Accent'.

On 'correctness' see MITTINS: WHAT IS CORRECTNESS? and MITTINS et al: ATTITUDES TO ENGLISH USAGE.

The relationship between language for living and language for learning will be discussed in more detail in DOUGHTY AND DOUGHTY: LANGUAGE AND COMMUNITY (in this series). The question of the place of language in the work of the English department, and the role of the English department in the curriculum, is considered in DOUGHTY: LANGUAGE, 'ENGLISH', AND THE CURRICULUM.

Two other books in this series consider specific areas of language work in school—ASHWORTH: LANGUAGE IN THE JUNIOR SCHOOL and HARRISON: ENGLISH AS A SECOND AND FOREIGN LANGUAGE. The latter has much to say about the teaching of immigrants.

For lecturers in Colleges of Education (Ed.) DENNIS: LANGUAGE STUDY IN TEACHER EDUCATION offers a number of suggestions as to the way in which courses of Language Study might be set up and fitted into college curricula.

Appendix

Language in Use, Exploring Language **and Language Study**

In this section we link together, in a selection of examples, units from *Language in Use*, chapters from *Exploring Language* and some of the literature to which they might lead. These examples are offered in order to illustrate ways in which components of a course in Language Study might be built up, beginning at points within the language and experience of the student and gradually leading on to explorations in the literature.

1. Language

Language in Use Units D1, D2, D3 and D4.

These units are concerned with, respectively, 'the internal organization of language, sounds, words and meanings, and how they inter-relate'; 'the . . . fact that language works because much of what we say is predictable'; 'what limits there are upon . . . (our) . . . freedom' to say what we want to say; and the way in which 'language is composed of many inter-related patterns'.

Exploring Language, chapter Nine—Spoken and Written.

This chapter looks at the nature of spoken language, and its relationship to written language.

FIRTH: 'The Problem of Meaning' in TONGUES OF MEN & SPEECH.

See, for example, p. 177 and the notion of 'pivotal points' of language, and their relationship to meaning.

FRY: 'SPEECH RECEPTION AND PERCEPTION'.

The early pages discuss 'the vast store of information' about language that has to be carried in the brain of any language user, the way in which this information has to be systematized and the way in which one has to be able to predict what other people are going to say if one is to understand them.

For an introduction to the way in which linguists describe the 'elements and structures' of language see references on p. 78.

Language in Use Units C6 and C7.

These units serve as an introduction to intonation, and (C7) the possibilities open to a language user of implying rather than making explicit what he means.

Exploring Language, chapter Nine.

HALLIDAY : INTONATION AND GRAMMAR IN BRITISH ENGLISH for a description of the intonation system in British English.

C7 ('Implications') might serve as an introduction to meaning in spoken language, language as code (see HASAN: 'REGISTER, CODE AND SOCIAL DIALECT'), the concept of 'meaning potential' and Halliday's use of the term 'socio-semantic' (see 'LANGUAGE IN A SOCIAL PERSPECTIVE' in HALLIDAY: EXPLORATIONS IN THE FUNCTIONS OF LANGUAGE).

2. Language and the individual

Language in Use, Unit C3.

This unit is concerned with the 'physical features which go to make up the uniqueness of a particular voice', called indexical features.

See ABERCROMBIE: ELEMENTS OF GENERAL PHONETICS for a phonetician's description.

Language in Use, Units F1, D7, D8.

These units are concerned with categories as language makes them available to the individual.

Exploring Language, chapter Four.

This chapter is concerned with the way in which experience is categorized by the language and the language-learner.

ABERCROMBIE : THE ANATOMY OF JUDGMENT, in which the author discusses the process of categorization.

DOUGLAS: PURITY AND DANGER.

Some categories, like those of cleanliness and dirtiness, are deeply significant for the life of the individual and for the life of society. Chapters 7 ('External Boundaries)', 8 '(Internal Lines') and 9 ('The System at War with Itself') consider the importance of boundaries between categories, and how they are maintained.

In his Introduction to CLASS, CODES AND CONTROL, Bernstein

records how Professor Douglas helped to focus his work 'upon the idea of the variable strength of boundaries and their relationship to the structuring and realizing of experience'. For an application of this to the educational world see BERNSTEIN: 'ON THE CLASSIFICATION AND FRAMING OF EDUCATIONAL KNOWLEDGE' in both CLASS, CODES and CONTROL and (Ed.) YOUNG: KNOWLEDGE AND CONTROL.

Language in Use, Units H3, H5, H6.
These units are concerned with various aspects of self.
Exploring Language, chapter Five.
This chapter, Language and Relationships, takes the argument further, and points towards BERGER: INVITATION TO SOCIOLOGY, and other works referenced at the end of the chapter.

GOFFMAN: STIGMA and THE PRESENTATION OF SELF IN EVERYDAY LIFE might well come in here, to be followed by a consideration of the theory of 'personal constructs'. See BANNISTER AND FRANSELLA: INQUIRING MAN and BRITTON: LANGUAGE AND LEARNING.

3. Language and culture

Language in Use, Unit F2.
The starting point of this unit is 'the fact that certain tasks are traditionally thought to be the prerogative of one sex or the other' and explores the way in which this is reflected in the language.

Exploring Language, chapter Three and THORNTON: THE INDIVIDUAL'S DEVELOPMENT OF HIS LANGUAGE look a little more deeply at culturally determined differences between male and female in society.

HUDSON: FRAMES OF MIND, chapter 3, 'Masculine and Feminine', points to some educational implications of this differentiation.

D'ANDRADE: 'SEX DIFFERENCES AND CULTURAL INSTITUTIONS' in (Ed.) HUDSON: THE ECOLOGY OF HUMAN INTELLIGENCE considers 'some of the very complex mechanisms that play a part in the development of sex differences in all human societies'.

Language in Use, Units H1 and H2, 'Family Names' and 'Personal Names', look at the part that names play in relationships.

Exploring Language, chapter Five, examines relationships more closely.

BERGER AND LUCKMANN: THE SOCIAL CONSTRUCTION OF REALITY argue, as their title implies, that what the individual comes to accept as reality is socially constructed, and they 'analyse the process in which this occurs'. In the chapter entitled 'Society as Subjective Reality' they say, of names that we are given, 'Every name implies a nomenclature, which in turn implies a designated social location'. This particular 'pathway' through the reading could usefully be linked with that suggested under the heading of 'self' in the previous section, and with the same authors' treatment of 'role' in THE SOCIAL CONSTRUCTION OF REALITY.

4. Language and society

Language in Use, Units J4 and J5.

Both units are concerned with the way in which language is used to establish and maintain contact with other people.

Exploring Language, chapters Five, Six and Eight.

Five and Six discuss, among other points, relationships in society. Chapter 8, part ii, begins to look at relationships in the class-room, and how such relationships constrain language. To take this further, see

BARNES: CLASSROOM CONTEXTS FOR LANGUAGE AND LEARNING and, on relationships in school, HANNAM, SMYTH AND STEPHENSON: YOUNG TEACHERS AND RELUCTANT LEARNERS.

Language in Use, Units C4 and F10.

One notion which may act as a constraint on the use of language is that of accent. These units may be used to begin a linguistic consideration of accent, and may be followed by *Exploring Language*, chapter Ten, 'Accent and Dialect'.

ABERCROMBIE : 'RP AND LOCAL ACCENT' in STUDIES IN PHONETICS AND LINGUISTICS is also very useful.

Language in Use, Units D6 and F9.

Allied to 'folk-linguistic' notions of accent and dialect may be notions of correctness. F9 explores the linguistic basis of 'popular notions of "corrections" ', and D6 looks at the kind of corrections made on pupils' written work. Grammatical notions of 'correctness' are examined in PALMER: GRAMMAR, section 1.3 'Correct and incorrect'. See also MITTINS: 'WHAT IS CORRECTNESS?' and MITTINS et al: ATTITUDES TO ENGLISH USAGE.

Language in Use, Units K1 and K2, 'Schools and colleges' and 'School traditions'.

These units may be used to begin a detailed look at school organization and structure.

Many of the excerpts in COSIN et al: SCHOOL AND SOCIETY will be helpful. See the Introduction, and the section introductions—especially that to section III, 'Learning and its organisation in school'.

Various aspects of school organization are touched upon in CREBER: LOST FOR WORDS. (How certain types of school organization help to educate for failure.)

LETTER TO TEACHER. (How some pupils start at a disadvantage and become more and more disadvantaged until they drop out altogether.)

HANNAM, SMYTH AND STEPHENSON: YOUNG TEACHERS AND RELUCTANT LEARNERS, chapter 4. (How young teachers have to fit into the authority structure of a school.)

Language in Use, Units E7 and G9.

E7, 'Write me an essay', tries to show how words used to describe tasks in school are 'a function of the social context provided by the school', while G9, 'The language of school subjects', 'considers the crucial part played by key terms in the understanding of new concepts'—especially as those concepts appear in school subjects.

Exploring Language, Chapter Seven, Command of a Language, 'is concerned with the way in which a speaker extends his command over spoken and written language'—particularly in the context of demands upon him in school.

DOUGHTY: LANGUAGE, 'English' and the curriculum takes the exploration further.

The study of the language of school subjects might now form the starting point for a look at the status of subjects within the curriculum. Especially helpful are various contributions to (Ed.) YOUNG: KNOWLEDGE AND CONTROL. (See references on p. 81.)

See also various contributions to (Ed.) HOOPER: THE CURRICULUM.

Bibliography

Abercrombie, D. *Studies in Phonetics and Linguistics* (O.U.P. 1965)
— *Elements of General Phonetics* (Edinburgh, 1967)
Abercrombie, M. L. J. *The Anatomy of Judgment* (Penguin, 1969)
Albrow, K. H. *The English Writing System* (Papers in Linguistics and English Teaching, Series 11, Longman, 1972)
Ashworth, E. *Language in the Junior School* (Edward Arnold, in this series, forthcoming)
Bannister, D. and Fransella, F. *Inquiring Man: The Theory of Personal Constructs* (Penguin, 1971)
Barnes, D. 'Classroom Contexts for Language and Learning' in *The Context of Language* (Educational Review, Birmingham University, 1971)
Barnes, D. and Britton, J. N. *Language, the learner and the school* (Penguin, 1969)
Berger, P. L. *Invitation to Sociology* (Penguin, 1966)
Berger, P. L. and Luckmann, T. *The Social Construction of Reality* (Penguin University Books, 1971)
Bernstein, B. *Class, Codes and Control, Vol. I* (Routledge and Kegan Paul, 1971)
(Ed.) Bernstein, B. *Class, Codes and Control, Vol. II* (Routledge and Kegan Paul, forthcoming)
Boomer, D. S. 'Hesitation Pausing and Grammatical Encoding' in (Ed.) Oldfield R. C. and Marshall J. C. *Language*
Britton, J. N. *Language and Learning* (Penguin 1972)
Chao, Y. R. *Language and Symbolic Systems* (C.U.P. 1968)
Cosin, B., Dale, I. R., Esland, G. M., Swift, D. F. *School and Society* (Routledge and Kegan Paul, 1971)
Creber, J. W. P. *Lost for Words* (Penguin, 1972)
Crystal, D. *Linguistics* (Penguin, 1971)
(Ed.) Dennis, G. W. *Language Study in Teacher Education* (Edward Arnold, in this series, forthcoming)

Doughty, P. S. *Language, 'English' and the curriculum.* (Papers in Linguistics
and English Teaching, Series 11, Longman, 1972)
Doughty, P. S. and E. A. *Language and Community* (Edward Arnold, in
this series, forthcoming)
Doughty, P. S., Pearce, J. J. and Thornton, G. M. *Language in Use*
(Edward Arnold, 1971)
— — — *Exploring Language* (Edward Arnold, 1972)
Doughty, P. S. and Thornton, G. M. *Command of a language: towards a
theory of competence in teaching and learning* (Papers in Linguistics and
English Teaching, Series 11, Longman, 1972)
Douglas, M. *Purity and Danger* (Penguin, 1970)
— *Natural Symbols* (Cresset Press, 1970)
Firth, J. R. *Papers in Linguistics,* 1934–51 (O.U.P. 1957)
— *The Tongues of Men & Speech* (O.U.P. 1964)
Frankenberg, R. *Communities in Britain* (Penguin, 1966)
Fry, D. B. 'Speech Reception and Perception' in (Ed.) Oldfield R. C.
and Marshall, J. C. *Language* (Penguin)
(Ed.) Giglioli, P. P. *Language and Social Context* (Penguin, 1972)
Goffman, E. *Stigma* (Penguin, 1967)
— *The Presentation of Self in Everyday Life* (Penguin, 1969)
Goldman Eisler, F. *Psycholinguistics* (Academic Press, N.Y., 1968)
Gregory, R. L. *The Intelligent Eye* (Weidenfeld and Nicholson, 1970)
Gurney, R. *Language, Brain and Interactive Processes* (Edward Arnold, in
this series, forthcoming)
Hall, E. T. *The Silent Language* (Doubleday, 1959)
Halliday, M. A. K. *Intonation and Grammar in British English* (Mouton,
1967)
— *Explorations in the Functions of Language* (Edward Arnold, in this
series)
— 'Language Structure and Language Function' in (Ed.) Lyons J.
New Horizons in Linguistics (Penguin)
— 'Learning how to mean' in (Ed.) Lenneberg, E. H. *Foundations of
Language: A Multidisciplinary Approach* (UNESCO and IBRO
forthcoming)
Hannam, C., Smyth, P. and Stephenson, N. *Young teachers and reluctant
learners* (Penguin, 1971)
Harrison, J. B. *English as a Second and Foreign Language* (Edward
Arnold, in this series)
Hasan, R. 'Register, Code and Social Dialect' in (Ed.) Bernstein, B.
Class, Codes and Control, Vol. II
(Ed.) Hooper, R. *The Curriculum* (Oliver and Boyd, 1971)
Hudson, L. *Contrary Imaginations* (Penguin, 1967)
— *Frames of Mind* (Penguin, 1970)
(Ed.) Hudson, L. *The Ecology of Human Intelligence* (Penguin, 1970)
Laver, J. 'The Production of Speech' in (Ed.) Lyons, J. *New Horizons
in Linguistics*

91

Lawton, D. *Social Class, Language and Education* (Routledge and Kegan Paul, 1968)
Lenneberg, E. H. *The Biological Foundations of Language* (Wiley, 1957)
— 'Speech as a motor skill with special reference to non-aphasic disorders' in (Ed.) Pribram, K. H. *Adaptations* (Penguin)
(Ed.) Lenneberg E. H. *New Directions in the Study of Language* (M.I.T. 1966)
Letter to a Teacher by the School of Barbiana (Penguin, 1970)
Lyons, J. *Introduction to Theoretical Linguistics* (C.U.P. 1968)
(Ed.) Lyons, J. *New Horizons in Linguistics* (Penguin, 1970)
Mackay, D., Thompson, B., Schaub, P. *Breakthrough to Literacy, Teachers' Manual* (Longman, 1970)
Medawar, P. B. *Induction and Intuition in Scientific Thought* (Methuen, 1969)
Mittins, W. H. 'What is correctness?' in *The State of Language* (Educational Review, University of Birmingham, Nov. 1969)
Mittins, W. H. et al. *Attitudes to English Usage* (O.U.P. 1970)
Nathan, P. *The Nervous System* (Penguin, 1969)
(Ed.) Oldfield, R. C. and Marshall, J. C. *Language* (Penguin, 1968)
Palmer, F. *Grammar* (Penguin, 1971)
Postman, N. and Weingartner, C. *Teaching as a Subversive Activity* (Penguin, 1971)
(Ed.) Pribram, K. H. *Adaptation* (Brain and Behaviour 4, Penguin Modern Psychology, 1969)
Pride, J. B. *The Social Meaning of Language* (O.U.P. 1971)
(Ed.) Richardson, K. and Spears, D. *Race, Culture and Intelligence* (Penguin, 1972)
(Ed.) Rubinstein, D. and Stoneman, C. *Education for Democracy* (Penguin, 1970)
Sapir, E. *Language* (Harcourt Brace & World Inc., 1921)
— *Culture, Language and Personality* (Univ. of California, 1949)
Sharp, D. *Language in Bi-lingual Communities* (Edward Arnold, in this series, forthcoming)
Sprott, W. J. H. *Human Groups* (Penguin, 1958)
Talland, G. A. *Disorders of Memory and Learning* (Penguin, 1968)
Thornton, G. M. *Language, Experience and School* (Edward Arnold, in this series, forthcoming)
— 'The Individual's Development of Language' in Thornton, G. M., Birk, D. and Hudson, R. A. *Language at Work* (Papers in Linguistics and English Teaching, Series 11, Longman, 1972)
Whorf, B. L. *Language, Thought and Reality* (Wiley, 1956)
Wilkinson, A. *The Foundations of Language* (O.U.P. 1971)
(Ed.) Wiseman, S. *Intelligence and Ability* (Penguin, 1967)
Wooldridge, D. *The Machinery of the Brain*, (McGraw Hill, 1960)
(Ed.) Young M. *Knowledge and Control* (Collier-MacMillan, 1971)